THE LEAST OF THE APOSTLES

THE MINISTRY AND LETTERS OF PAUL

IN CHRONOLOGICAL ORDER

DENNIS E. INGOLFSLAND, DPHIL

AN IMPRINT OF
GLOBALEDADVANCEPRESS
WWW.GLOBALEDADVANCE.ORG

THE LEAST OF THE APOSTLES
–The Ministry and Letters of Paul in Chronological Order

Copyright © 2009 by Dennis Ingolfsland

Library of Congress Control Number: 2009928349

Ingolfsland, Dennis, 1954–

ISBN 978-1-935434-22-1

Subject Codes and Description: 1. REL 006070 Religion
– Biblical Commentary -- New Testament; 2. REL 006220 –
RELIGION—BIBLICAL Studies – New Testament;; 3. REL 006630
– Religion -=- Biblical Studies – history and Culture.

The translation used was the NetBible, an excellent internet
translation done by reputable scholars.
—Used by Permission

Cover photograph taken by the author:
Archaelogical remains of steps leading up to the
Temple mount in Jerusalem

Printed in the United States of America

Published by
Post-Gutenberg Books™
An imprint of
GlobalEdAdvance Press
globaledadvance.org

DEDICATED TO MY FAMILY:

TO SHEILA,
MY DEVOTED WIFE OF 35 YEARS;

TO MY WONDERFUL CHILDREN
AND CHILDREN-IN-LAW:
KEVIN AND SARAH,
MELINDA AND CHRIS,
JASON AND GEORGIA;

TO MY ADORABLE GRANDCHILDREN,
LUCY, SAWYER AND WYATT,
AND IN MEMORY OF AIDEN.

C O N T E N T S

INTRODUCTION   11
     Paul in a nutshell   12
     Historical Background   15

Chapter 1:   19
FROM PAUL'S CONVERSION TO THE JERUSALEM COUNCIL

     The conversion of Saul / Paul   19
     Paul's first missionary journey   21
     Introduction to Galatians   26

Chapter 2:
PAUL'S SECOND MISSIONARY JOURNEY   35

     Introduction to First Thessalonians   40
     Introduction to Second Thessalonians   44

Chapter 3:
PAUL'S THIRD MISSIONARY JOURNEY: 47
First Corithians

     Introduction to First Corinthians   49

Chapter 4:
PAUL'S THIRD MISSIONARY JOURNEY: 65
Second Corinthians

     Introduction to the "harsh letter"   65
     Paul's Third Missionary Journey Cont.   69
     Introduction to Second Corinthians   71

Chapter 5;   79
PAUL'S THIRD MISSIONARY JOURNEY:
Romans
    Introduction to Romans   79

Chapter 6:
FROM CORINTH TO JERUSALEM TO ROME   99

    From Corinth to Jerusalem   99
    Paul's arrest in Jerusalem   101
    Paul's imprisonment in Caesarea   105
    Paul's voyage to Rome   109
    Paul's imprisonment in Rome   112
    Historical Background   113

Chapter 7:   115
PAUL'S PRISON LETTERS: Ephesians

    Introduction to Ephesians   115

Chapter 8:   123
PAUL'S PRISON LETTERS: Philippians

    Introduction to Philippians   123

Chapter 9:   129
PAUL'S PRISON LETTERS:
Colossian and Philemon

    Introduction to Colossians   129
    Introduction to Philemon   135

Chapter 10   137
PASTORAL EPISTLES: Titus

    Introduction to Pastoral Epistles   137

Chapter 11   141
PASTORAL EPISTLES: First Timothy

Chapter 12:   147
PASTORAL EPISTLES: Second Timothy

§

APPENDIX ONE: 153
After Paul

APPENDIX TWO: 155
Paul's Letters and the New Testament Canon

    Second Peter   155
    Clement of Rome   156
    Ignatius   157
    Polycarp   157
    Irenaeus   158

APPENDIX THREE: 163
Jesus and Paul

    The Christology of Jesus   163
    The Soteriology of Jesus   167
    The Ethics of Jesus   174
    Other Parallels   176
    Conclusion   178

APPENDIX FOUR:
Works Cited   179

ABOUT THE AUTHOR   181

INTRODUCTION

In the early 1500's Michelangelo spent four years painting a 5,000 square foot masterpiece on the ceiling of Sistine chapel in the Vatican. Imagine that you've spent years studying this painting—but have never seen it from more than twelve inches away! You might have a great appreciation for the detail, the colors, the brush strokes—but you've never seen the big picture!

Regrettably, that is the only way many Christians have seen the Bible. They may read a verse or even a chapter as part of their daily devotions, but many Christians have never read an entire New Testament book in one sitting. They may know a lot of verses, but they don't have a grasp on the big picture.

Unfortunately, without knowing the big picture, it is often hard to interpret the verses accurately. As a result, even well-meaning Christians sometimes come up with bizarre interpretations of the Bible by "cherry picking" verses, ripping them from their contexts, and interpreting them in ways that the biblical author would never have intended. Many Christians get "tossed to and fro" by every new fad coming down the pike because they don't know the big picture.

The purpose of this book is to provide the "big picture" of a large part of the New Testament: Paul's ministry and letters. Over 7,000 books have been published about Paul. This one is different. It consists almost entirely of Paul in his own words, placed in the context provided by Luke, one of Paul's earliest associates.

In this book, Paul's letters have been placed chronologically (in italics) within the story of his ministry as recorded by Luke in the Book of Acts. Paul's letters and the story of Paul's ministry have been carefully condensed by removing repeated ideas, extra words, or minor clauses. While most of what Paul wrote in his letters has been retained, the speeches in the book of Acts have been considerably shortened to provide the gist of what each speaker said. The result allows the reader to get the big picture of Paul's message and ministry in a relatively short period of time. The translation chosen for this project was the NetBible, an excellent scholarly translation, used by permission and available on the web at:

http://www.bible.org/netbible/index.htm

It is worth emphasizing, however, that in the process of condensing the material, important minor points, arguments, and supporting quotations from the Old Testament have often been condensed or omitted, *so this book should not be used as a substitute for the New Testament.* The book will provide the big picture of Paul's ministry and message, but for a more accurate, detailed, and serious study of Paul's message, the reader must go to the New Testament itself.

Paul in a nutshell

For those who have little or no knowledge of Paul's ministry and message, the following short summary may provide a helpful introduction:

The story actually starts with Jesus. Jesus was a first century Jew who was crucified in AD 30 or 33 by the Roman governor, Pontius Pilate, at the instigation of some Jewish religious leaders. Jesus was executed, not just because he claimed to be the Jewish Messiah, but because he claimed to do things that, in a Jewish culture, only God could do. For example according to the Gospels, he claimed to have authority over the Sabbath Day, authority to nullify biblical dietary laws, and authority to directly forgive people's sins. In a first century Jewish context (and context is everything!) only God was above Sabbath and the dietary laws, and only God could forgive people's sins. The Gospel of John even records that Jesus claimed God was his "father" and that he was one with God.

While most people rejected Jesus' extravagant claims, his followers believed in him not just because of the power of his message, but because 1) they were convinced that he had really fulfilled ancient Jewish prophecies, 2) they believed he had performed amazing miracles which no one had ever done before, and 3) they were absolutely convinced that Jesus physically rose from the dead after his execution! (We might also add that his prophecy about the destruction of the Jewish temple literally came true just 40 years after his death and resurrection).

Some of Jesus' contemporaries, however, thought Jesus was insane or demon possessed and that his claims were "blasphemy." Since blasphemy was a sin punishable by death, they arranged to have Jesus executed. Shortly after Jesus' death by crucifixion, however, his followers claimed to have seen, heard and touched Jesus who was very much alive! In fact, they even claimed to have eaten meals with him! Severe persecution did not dissuade them from bearing witness to what they had seen and heard. As a result, thousands came to believe in Jesus as Savior and Lord.

One man who was not persuaded at first was a promising young Jewish leader named Saul. He had been trained under a prominent Jewish rabbi named Gamaliel and was zealous for his Jewish faith. Saul persecuted Christians severely until one day he was on his way to Damascus to arrest Christians when he saw a blinding light and heard the voice of Jesus! Although this was a vision of sorts, it was not entirely subjective since according to the Book of Acts, the others with Saul also saw the light and heard the voice, even though they didn't understand it.[1] This experience changed Saul's life forever. He even changed his name from Saul to Paul.

After three years in Arabia sorting it all out, Paul began preaching the Good News that Jesus was the long awaited Jewish Messiah, Savior and Son of God who had died as an atoning sacrifice to save us from the penalty of our sins.

Paul taught that this salvation was only available by the grace of God to those who turn in repentance and faith to Jesus as their Savior and Lord. Paul insisted that this salvation was *not* available to those who thought they were good enough to earn it. Furthermore, Paul taught that this salvation was available not only to his fellow Jews but to believers of every nationality and race.

This was a pretty radical idea to many of Paul's Jewish peers and Paul's ministry was often very unpopular. As a result of intense persecution, Paul was sometimes beaten, jailed, rejected, run out of town, shipwrecked, and once, even stoned with real stones! Yet, like the commercial about the "Energizer bunny," he just kept going and going and going. He was so convinced that Jesus really was the physically risen Son of God that absolutely nothing could dissuade him from his mission.

Paul, therefore, traveled from his base church in Antioch (in modern Lebanon) to towns all over the Roman provinces of Galatia, Asia, Macedonia and Achaia (regions in what we would today call Turkey and Greece) preaching this good news or "gospel," converting people to Jesus, and establishing churches. He then wrote several letters to these churches addressing specific issues that had come up. Although some of these letters have been lost, twelve of them have been collected in the New Testament.

Paul was not intending to start a new religion. He believed Jesus was the long awaited messiah that Jewish

---

1   Acts 22:6-9.

prophets had predicted, and Paul was convinced that he was just proclaiming Jesus and Jesus' message.

Historical Background

It may be helpful to know something about the historical background of the times in which Paul lived and ministered. The events in chapter one below took place in the 30's and 40's AD when Herod Antipas was ruling Galilee. Herod Antipas, the son of Herod the Great (who had tried to kill the baby Jesus), was ruling when both John the Baptist and Jesus were executed.

Antipas had divorced his wife in order to marry his half-brother's wife. Unfortunately for Herod Antipas, the wife he divorced was the daughter of King Aretas who ruled a kingdom on the west side of the Jordan River. King Aretas was not pleased that his daughter would be treated this way. He spent the next several years raising an army to attack Herod! The attack finally came in AD 36—about six years after Jesus' death—during which Aretas nearly wiped out Herod's whole army. By this time, however, Paul was back in his hometown of Tarsus, far away from the war.

Also in AD 36, a fire destroyed the "Circus Maximus" in Rome. Romans, like people today, loved their entertainment so they were infuriated when Emperor Tiberius refused to rebuilt their stadium. Tiberius had also placed restrictions on other entertainments and luxury goods so the people were thrilled in the following year at the news that Tiberius had died at the ripe old age of 78. The Roman Senate immediately called a meeting and prayed to the gods to send Tiberius' soul to hell (and you thought today's politicians were harsh)!

Tiberius' heir was Gaius Julius Caesar Germanicus, better known by his nick-name, "Caligula," meaning, "Little Boots." Caligula was known for his vicious brutality. He became convinced that he was a god and he sometimes tried to make himself appear like popular images of the god Jupiter. In AD 38 after ordering his engineers to construct a bridge of boats so he could walk across the water. He claimed that he had conquered Neptune, the god of the sea.

Caligula then gave orders that a statue of himself should be set up in a Jewish synagogue in Alexandria, Egypt. The Jewish population of Alexandria rioted in protest and by the time the riots were put down, hundreds of Jews lay dead.

Caligula then decided to have his statue set up in the great Jewish Temple in Jerusalem. By this time Herod Antipas had died and had been succeeded by his son, Herod Agrippa I. It was Herod Agrippa I who put Peter in prison and executed the apostle James (not to be confused with James, the half brother of Jesus who was one of the leaders of the early church). When Agrippa I rose to power, the province of Judea was added to his kingdom by his friend, Caligula. Judea was where Jerusalem and the Jewish Temple were located.

Herod Agrippa I was a wise enough politician to know that trying to set up a statue in the Jewish Temple could result in all-out war, so he begged Caligula not to do it. This attempt severely strained their friendship but Caligula would not back down. As it turned out, Caligula was assassinated before the statue could be delivered. When the Roman commander in Judea heard of Caligula's death, he refused to carry out the command.

Herod Agrippa I died a few years later in AD 44 during a celebration in Caesarea when the sun reflected off his dazzling metallic robe and the crowds were hailing him as a god. Agrippa knew better than to accept worship as a god, but he did nothing to stop the people. According to the Book of Acts and the Jewish historian Josephus, Agrippa suddenly became fatally ill and died shortly thereafter. Only a few years later, Paul and Barnabas would be hailed as Greek gods by the people in Lystra. Unlike Agrippa, Paul and Barnabas protested strongly when the people tried to worship them.

Caligula was succeeded in AD 41 by his uncle Claudius who had a reputation for being something of a buffoon. He was socially inept, eccentric, absent minded, and was sometimes even known to drool. Nevertheless, he was also a conscientious, intelligent and a trained historian. The Roman Senate was not sure what to do with him but since he had the support of the Praetorian Guard and threatened to use force, they appointed him emperor.[2]

As we will see below, while all this was going on, the church in Antioch (in modern Lebanon) was booming! The church in Jerusalem sent Barnabas to pastor the Antioch church, and Barnabas went to Tarsus to persuade Paul to help him. It wasn't long before the church in Antioch sent Paul and Barnabas on their first missionary journey. As we have seen, Paul's world, like ours, could be a very dangerous place.

What follows is the story of this remarkable man—a man absolutely committed to Jesus Christ— taken entirely from the original sources as translated in the NetBible.

2   Klingaman, William K. The First Century. New York : Harper-Perennial, 1991, 205-232, 239-253

CHAPTER ONE

From Paul's Conversion to the Jerusalem Council

The Conversion of Saul / Paul[3] (early 30's AD)

"You stubborn people! You are heathen at heart and deaf to the truth. Must you forever resist the Holy Spirit? Your ancestors did and so do you! They even killed the ones who predicted the coming of the Messiah whom you betrayed and murdered."

The Jewish leaders were infuriated by Stephen's accusation. But Stephen, full of the Holy Spirit, gazed steadily upward into heaven and told them, "Look, I see the heavens opened and the Son of Man[4] standing in the place of honor at God's right hand!"

They rushed him, dragged him out of the city and began to stone him. The official witnesses took off their coats and laid them at the feet of a young man named Saul. As they stoned him, Stephen prayed, "Lord Jesus, receive my spirit, don't charge them with this sin!" With that, he died.

Saul was one of the official witnesses at the killing of Stephen. A great wave of persecution began that day, sweeping over the church in Jerusalem, and believers, except the apostles, fled into Judea and Samaria. Saul was going everywhere to devastate the church. He went from house to

---

3   From Acts 7-9.

4   Jesus often referred to himself as the "Son of Man."

house, dragging out both men and women to throw them into jail.

Saul was eager to destroy the Lord's followers so he went to the high priest. He requested letters addressed to the synagogues in Damascus asking their cooperation in the arrest of any followers of the Way.[5] As he was nearing Damascus on this mission, a brilliant light from heaven suddenly beamed down upon him! He fell to the ground and heard a voice saying to him, "Saul! Saul! Why are you persecuting me?"

"Who are you, sir?" Saul asked.

"I am Jesus, the one you are persecuting! Now get up and go into the city, and you will be told what to do."

As Saul picked himself up off the ground, he was blind. His companions led him to Damascus.

Now there was a believer in Damascus named Ananias. The Lord spoke to him in a vision, calling, "Ananias!" Go over to Straight Street to the house of Judas. When you arrive, ask for Saul of Tarsus."

"But Lord," exclaimed Ananias, "I've heard about the terrible things this man has done to the believers in Jerusalem! We hear that he is authorized by the leading priests to arrest every believer in Damascus."

The Lord said, "Go, for Saul is my chosen instrument to take my message to the Gentiles and to kings, as well as to the people of Israel. I will show him how much he must suffer for me."

So Ananias found Saul. He laid his hands on him and said, "Brother Saul, the Lord Jesus, who appeared to you on the road, has sent me so that you may get your sight back and be filled with the Holy Spirit." Instantly he regained his sight, got up, and was baptized. Saul stayed with the believers in Damascus for a few days and he began preaching about

---

5   The earliest Christians were known as followers of "The Way" before they were known as "Christians."

Jesus in the synagogues, saying, "He is indeed the Son of God!"

All who heard him were amazed. "Isn't this the same man who persecuted Jesus' followers with such devastation in Jerusalem?" they asked. "We understand that he came here to arrest them and take them in chains to the leading priests."

Saul's preaching became more and more powerful, and the Jews in Damascus couldn't refute his proofs that Jesus was indeed the Messiah. The Jewish leaders decided to kill him but during the night some believers let him down in a large basket through an opening in the city wall.

When Saul arrived in Jerusalem he tried to meet with the believers but they were afraid of him. Then Barnabas brought him to the apostles and told them how Saul had seen the Lord on the way to Damascus and how Saul boldly preached in the name of Jesus there.

Then the apostles accepted Saul and he was with them in Jerusalem, preaching boldly in the name of the Lord. debated with some Greek-speaking Jews, but they plotted to murder him. When the believers heard about it, however, they took him to Caesarea and sent him on to his hometown of arsus. The church then had peace throughout Judea, Galilee, and Samaria, and it grew in strength and numbers.

Paul's First missionary journey[6]

The believers who had fled from Jerusalem during the persecution which arose after Stephen's death traveled as far as Phoenicia, Cyprus, and Antioch of Syria. Some believers who went to Antioch from Cyprus and Cyrene began preaching to Gentiles about Jesus and large numbers of these Gentiles believed.

When the church at Jerusalem heard what had

---

6   From Acts 11, 13-15.

happened, they sent Barnabas to Antioch. [7] Barnabas was a good man, full of the Holy Spirit and strong in faith, and large numbers of people were brought to the Lord.

Barnabas went to Tarsus to find Saul and brought him back to Antioch. Both of them stayed there with the church for a full year teaching great numbers of people (It was at Antioch that the believers were first called Christians).

During this time, some prophets traveled from Jerusalem to Antioch. One of them named Agabus stood up in one of the meetings to predict by the Spirit that a great famine was coming upon the entire Roman world (This was fulfilled during the reign of Claudius).[8]

The believers in Antioch decided to send relief to the brothers and sisters in Judea, entrusting their gifts to Barnabas and Saul to take to the elders of the church in

Jerusalem.

When Barnabas and Saul had finished their mission in Jerusalem they returned to Antioch, taking John Mark with them. Among the prophets and teachers of the church

---

7   Historical Background: Antioch in Syria (not to be confused with Antioch of Pisidia) was not some little out-of-the-way village. The first century Jewish historian, Josephus, said it was the third city in the Roman Empire, right after Rome and Alexandria. The population was estimated to be as high as 500,000 and was very diverse, with Greeks, Jews, Persians, and even some people from China and India. The city had been founded over 300 years earlier by a general of Alexander the Great. It was apparently a very beautiful city with fountains, trees and double colonnades of pillars along a long boulevard paved with stones. Stott, John. *The Message of Acts.* Downers Grove, IL : Intervarsity Press, 1994, 203.

8   Historical Background: Several years later, when Paul writes to the Galatians, he says that after fourteen years (probably after his conversion) he went to Jerusalem with Titus "because of a revelation." Some scholars think that the revelation he is talking about is this revelation about the famine given by Agabus. It was at this time, Paul says, that he met with the "Pillars" of the Jerusalem Church, Peter, James and John, and they gave him their blessing to preach his gospel to the Gentiles.

at Antioch were Barnabas, Simeon (called "the black man"), Lucius (from Cyrene), Manaen (the childhood companion of King Herod Antipas), and Saul.

One day as these men were worshiping the Lord and fasting, the Holy Spirit said, "Dedicate Barnabas and Saul for the special work I have for them." After more fasting and prayer, the men laid their hands on them and sent them on their way.

Sent out by the Holy Spirit, Saul and Barnabas sailed for the island of Cyprus. There, in the town of Salamis, they went to the Jewish synagogues and preached the word of God (John Mark went with them as their assistant). Afterward they preached from town to town across the entire island until finally they reached Paphos where they met a Jewish sorcerer named Bar-Jesus. He had attached himself to the governor, Sergius Paulus.

The governor invited Barnabas and Saul to visit him for he wanted to hear the word of God. But the sorcerer was trying to turn the governor away from the Christian faith. Saul, also known as Paul, filled with the Holy Spirit, looked the sorcerer in the eye and said,

"You son of the Devil, full of every sort of trickery and villainy, enemy of all that is good, will you never stop perverting the true ways of the Lord? The Lord has laid his hand of punishment upon you and you will be stricken awhile with blindness."

Instantly darkness fell upon him and he began begging for someone to lead him. When the governor saw what had happened he believed and was astonished at what he learned about the Lord. Now Paul and those with him left Paphos by ship for Pamphylia, landing at the port town of Perga. There John Mark left them and returned to Jerusalem.

Barnabas and Paul traveled inland to Antioch of Pisidia. On the Sabbath they went to the synagogue for the services and after the usual readings from the books of Moses and the Prophets, those in charge of the service sent them this message: "Brothers, if you have any word of encouragement for us, come and give it!" So Paul stood started speaking:

People of Israel and devout Gentiles who fear the God of Israel: One of King David's descendants, Jesus, is God's promised Savior of Israel! The people in Jerusalem and their leaders fulfilled prophecy by condemning Jesus to death. They didn't realize that he is the one the prophets had written about. They found no just cause to execute him, but they asked Pilate to have him killed anyway. But God raised him from the dead! He appeared over a period of many days to those who had gone with him from Galilee to Jerusalem. In this man Jesus there is forgiveness for your sins. Everyone who believes in him is freed from all guilt and declared right with God.

As Paul and Barnabas left the synagogue that day the people asked them to return again and speak about these things the next week. The following week almost the entire city turned out to hear them preach. When the Jewish leaders saw the crowds they slandered Paul and argued against whatever he said.

Then Paul and Barnabas spoke out boldly and declared, "It was necessary that this Good News from God be given first to you Jews. But since you have rejected it and judged yourselves unworthy of eternal life, we will offer it to Gentiles."[9] When the Gentiles heard this, they thanked the Lord for his message; and all who were appointed to eternal life became believers. So the Lord's message spread throughout that region.

Then the Jewish leaders incited a mob against Paul and Barnabas and ran them out of town. They shook off the dust of their feet against them and went to the city of Iconium.

---

9   Gentiles are anyone who is not Jewish.

In Iconium, Paul and Barnabas went to the synagogue and preached with such power that a great number of both Jews and Gentiles believed. But the Jews who spurned God's message stirred up distrust among the Gentiles against Paul and Barnabas, saying all sorts of evil things about them. The apostles stayed there a long time preaching boldly about the grace of the Lord. The Lord proved their message was true by giving them power to do miraculous signs and wonders but the people of the city were divided in their opinion about them.

A mob of Gentiles and Jews decided to attack and stone them. When the apostles learned of it, they fled for their lives to the cities of Lystra and Derbe and the surrounding area, and they preached the Good News there.

While they were at Lystra, Paul and Barnabas came upon a man with crippled feet. Paul called to him, "Stand up!" The man jumped to his feet and started walking. When the crowd saw what Paul had done, they shouted, "These men are gods!" They decided that Barnabas was the Greek god Zeus and that Paul, because he was the chief speaker, was Hermes.

The temple of Zeus was located on the outskirts of the city. The priest of the temple and the crowd prepared to sacrifice to the apostles! Barnabas and Paul ran out among the people, shouting,

"Friends, we are merely human beings! We have come to bring you the Good News that you should turn from these worthless things to the living God, who made heaven and earth and everything in them."

Now some Jews arrived from Antioch and Iconium and turned the crowds into a murderous mob. They stoned Paul and dragged him out of the city, apparently dead, but as the believers stood around him he got up and went back into the city. The next day he and Barnabas left for Derbe.

After preaching the Good News in Derbe and making many disciples, Paul and Barnabas returned again to Lystra, Iconium, and Antioch of Pisidia where they strengthened the believers. They encouraged them to continue in the faith, reminding them that they must enter into the Kingdom of God through many tribulations. Paul and Barnabas also appointed elders in every church and prayed for them with fasting, turning them over to the care of the Lord.

Then they traveled back through Pisidia to Pamphylia and finally returned by ship to Antioch of Syria where their journey had begun. They called the church together and reported about their trip, telling all that God had done and how he had opened the door of faith to the Gentiles, too. They stayed with the believers in Antioch for a long time.

While Paul and Barnabas were at Antioch of Syria, some men from Judea arrived and began to teach the Christians: "Unless you keep the ancient Jewish custom of circumcision taught by Moses, you cannot be saved." Paul and Barnabas, disagreeing with them, argued forcefully and at length.

Introduction to Galatians

Even the most skeptical scholars agree Galatians was written by Paul some time between AD 48 and AD 56. One theory is that these "men from Judea" (above) had stopped off in Antioch after coming through Paul's brand new churches in Iconium, Lystra and Derbe, which were in the Roman province of Galatia.

These "men from Judea" were teaching that "Unless you keep the ancient Jewish custom of circumcision taught by Moses, you cannot be saved." When Paul heard this he was furious and was concerned that his new churches had been misled by this false teaching. As a result, he wrote his letter to his Galatian churches to correct the errors spread by these wandering teachers. If this theory is correct, Galatians was probably written around AD 48. Here is the essence of Paul's letter to the Galatians.

From Paul, an apostle (not from men but by Jesus Christ and God who raised him from the dead) and all the brothers with me, to the churches of Galatia. Grace and peace to you from God the Father and our Lord Jesus Christ, who gave himself for our sins to rescue us from this present evil age!

I am astonished that you are so quickly following a different gospel – not that there really is another gospel, but there are some who wanting to distort the gospel of Christ. If any one is preaching a gospel contrary to what you received, let him be condemned to hell! I want you to know, brothers and sisters that the gospel I preached is not of human origin. I received it by a revelation of Jesus Christ.

You have heard of how I was savagely persecuting the church and trying to destroy it. I was advancing in Judaism beyond many of my contemporaries and was extremely zealous for the traditions of my ancestors. But when the one who called me by his grace was pleased to reveal his Son in me, I did not ask advice from any human being but I departed to Arabia, and then returned to Damascus.

Then after three years I went up to Jerusalem to visit Cephas[10] and get information from him, and I stayed with him fifteen days. I saw none of the other apostles except James the Lord's brother. I assure you, before God, I am not lying! Afterward I went to the regions of Syria and Cilicia, but I was personally unknown to the churches of Judea. They were only hearing, "The one who once persecuted us is now proclaiming the good news of the faith he once tried to destroy."

Then after fourteen years I went up to Jerusalem again with Barnabas, taking Titus along too. I went there because of a revelation and presented to them the gospel that I preach among the Gentiles. Yet not even Titus was compelled to be circumcised, although he was a Greek.

---

10   The nickname Jesus gave to his disciple, Simon "Peter." Both Cephas and Peter (Petros) are words meaning "rock."

James,[11] Cephas, and John, who had a reputation as pillars, gave to Barnabas and me the right hand of fellowship, agreeing that we would go to the Gentiles and they to the circumcised. They requested only that we remember the poor, the very thing I also was eager to do.

But when Cephas came to Antioch I opposed him to his face, because he had clearly done wrong. Until certain people came from James, he had been eating with the Gentiles. But when they arrived, he stopped doing this because he was afraid of those who were pro-circumcision.[12] The rest of the Jews also joined him so that even Barnabas was led astray by their hypocrisy. When I saw that they were not behaving consistently with the truth of the gospel, I said to Cephas in front of them all,

"If you, a Jew, live like a Gentile, how can you try to force the Gentiles to live like Jews?" We are Jews by birth yet we know that no one is justified by the works of the law but by the faithfulness of Jesus Christ.

I have been crucified with Christ and it is no longer I who live, but Christ lives in me. So the life I now live, I live because of the faithfulness of the Son of God who loved me and gave himself for me.

You foolish Galatians! Did you receive the Spirit by doing the works of the law or by believing what you heard? Are you so foolish? Although you began with the Spirit, are you now trying to finish by human effort? Have you suffered so many things for nothing? – if indeed it was for nothing. Does God give you the Spirit and work miracles among you by your doing the works of the law or by your believing what you heard?

Abraham **believed God, and it was credited to him as**

---

11   One of Jesus' half-brothers.
12   In other words, those who thought circumcision was necessary in order to be saved.

righteousness,[13] *those who believe are the sons of Abraham. The scripture, foreseeing that God would justify the Gentiles by faith, proclaimed the gospel to Abraham saying, "**All the nations will be blessed in you.**" Those who believe are blessed along with Abraham the believer.*

*Christ redeemed us from the curse of the law by becoming a curse for us (because it is written, "**Cursed is everyone who hangs on a tree**") in order that in Christ Jesus the blessing of Abraham would come to the Gentiles by faith.*

Brothers and sisters, the promises were spoken to Abraham and to his descendant, referring to Christ. In Christ Jesus you are all sons of God through faith. There is neither Jew nor Greek, slave nor free, male nor female –all of you are one in Christ Jesus. If you belong to Christ, you are Abraham's descendants, heirs according to the promise.

When the appropriate time had come, God sent his Son to redeem those who were under the law, so that we may be adopted as sons with full rights. Because you are sons, God sent the Spirit of his Son into our hearts, who calls "Abba! Father!" You are no longer a slave but a son and an heir through God.

Now that you have come to know God (or rather to be known by God), how can you turn back again? Do you want to be enslaved all over again? You are observing religious days and months and seasons and years. I fear for you that my work for you may have been in vain.

You know it was because of a physical illness that I first proclaimed the gospel to you, and you did not despise or reject me. If it were possible, you would have pulled out your eyes and given them to me! Have I become your enemy by telling you the truth? My children –I wish I could be with you now and change my tone of voice, because I am perplexed about you.

---

13   Passages in bold are quotations from the Old Testament.

Christ has set us free. Stand firm, then, and do not be subject again to the yoke of slavery. Listen! I, Paul, tell you that if you let yourselves be circumcised, Christ will be of no benefit to you! You who are trying to be declared righteous by the law have been alienated from Christ; you have fallen away from grace! In Christ Jesus neither circumcision nor uncircumcision carries any weight – the only thing that matters is faith working through love.

*You were running well; who prevented you from obeying the truth? I wish those agitators would castrate themselves! You were called to freedom, brothers and sisters; only do not use your freedom as an opportunity to indulge your flesh, but through love serve one another. The whole law can be summed up in a single commandment, namely, "**You must love your neighbor as yourself.**"*

Live by the Spirit and you will not carry out the desires of the flesh. The works of the flesh are obvious: sexual immorality, impurity, depravity, idolatry, sorcery, hostilities, trife, jealousy, outbursts of anger, selfish rivalries, dissensions, factions, envying, murder, drunkenness, carousing, and similar things.[14] *Those who practice such things will not inherit the kingdom of God!*

But the fruit of the Spirit is love, joy, peace, patience, kindness, goodness, faithfulness, gentleness, and self-control. Those who belong to Christ have crucified the flesh with its passions and desires. If we live by the Spirit, let us also behave in accordance with the Spirit. Let us not become conceited, provoking one another, being jealous of one another.

If a person is discovered in some sin, you who are spiritual restore such a person in a spirit of gentleness. Pay close attention to yourselves so that you are not tempted too. Carry one another's burdens, and in this way you will fulfill the law of Christ. Let each one examine his own work. Then

---

14   Jesus also condemned such sins. See Mark 7:21-23.

he can take pride in himself and not compare himself with someone else.

The one who receives instruction in the word must share all good things with the one who teaches it. Do not be deceived. God will not be made a fool. A person will reap what he sows, because the person who sows to his own flesh will reap corruption from the flesh, but the one who sows to the Spirit will reap eternal life from the Spirit. So then, whenever we have an opportunity, do good to all people, especially to those who belong to the family of faith.

See what big letters I make as I write to you with my own hand! Those who want to make a good showing are trying to force you to be circumcised. Neither circumcision nor uncircumcision counts for anything; the only thing that matters is a new creation! All who will behave in accordance with this rule, peace and mercy be on them, and on the Israel of God.

The grace of our Lord Jesus Christ be with your spirit, brothers and sisters. Amen.

Paul and Barnabas were sent to Jerusalem,[15] accompanied by some local believers, to talk to the apostles

---

15   The conflict between Paul's teaching of salvation by grace and the teaching of these "men from Judea" led to significant controversy. It may have been at this time that James, the half-brother of Jesus and leader of the church in Jerusalem, also sent a letter out to the churches arguing that "Faith without works is dead" and that Abraham was saved by works when he offered up Isaac on the altar. This seemed to contradict what Paul was teaching and the controversy became so significant that Paul and Barnabas were sent to Jerusalem to discuss the issue. As it turned out, Paul and James were just looking at the issue from different angles. Paul was looking at faith as the source of works while James was looking at works as the evidence that comes from faith. Both agreed that genuine faith produces works. As seen below, they discovered their agreement when Barnabas and Paul went up to Jerusalem in AD 49 to meet with the apostles, a meeting later scholars would call, "The Jerusalem Council."

and elders about this question.[16] They were welcomed by the whole church, including the apostles and elders.

They reported on what God had been doing through their ministry. Then some of the men who had been Pharisees before their conversion stood up and declared that all Gentile converts must be circumcised and be required to follow the Law of Moses. After a long discussion, Peter stood and addressed them:

"Brothers, you all know that God chose me from among you some time ago to preach to the Gentiles so that they could hear the Good News and believe. God confirmed that he accepts Gentiles by giving them the Holy Spirit just as he gave him to us for he also cleansed their hearts through faith. We believe that we are all saved the same way, by the special favor of the Lord Jesus."

Everyone listened as Barnabas and Paul told about the miraculous signs and wonders God had done through them among the Gentiles. When they had finished, James stood and said,

"Brothers, Peter has told you about the time God first visited the Gentiles to take from them a people for himself. This conversion of Gentiles agrees with what the prophets predicted so my judgment is that we should stop troubling the Gentiles who turn to God, except that we should write to them and tell them to abstain from eating meat sacrificed to idols, from sexual immorality, and from consuming blood or eating the meat of strangled animals."

Then the apostles and elders and the whole church in Jerusalem chose delegates and sent them to Antioch of Syria with Paul and Barnabas to report on this decision.[17] The men

16   The question about whether Gentiles had to obey Jewish laws, particularly the law regarding circumcision, in order to be saved.

17   In the same year this council in Jerusalem was meeting, the Roman Emperor Claudius married his own niece, Agrippina, a 59 year old woman with an obsession for money and power. She persuaded Claudius to adopt her twelve year old son, Nero, and arranged to have

chosen were two of the church leaders, Judas (also called Barsabbas) and Silas.

The four messengers went to Antioch where they delivered the letter. Then Judas and Silas, both being prophets, spoke extensively to the Christians, encouraging and strengthening their faith. They stayed for a while, and then Judas and Silas were sent back to Jerusalem, with the blessings of the Christians. Paul and Barnabas stayed in Antioch to assist many others who were teaching and preaching the word of the Lord there.

---

him educated by Seneca, one of the best philosophers in Rome. Nero would later become the emperor to whom Paul would appeal when he appealed to Caesar.

CHAPTER TWO:

Paul's Second Missionary Journey[18]

After some time Paul said to Barnabas, "Let's return to each city where we previously preached the word of the Lord, to see how the new believers are getting along." Barnabas agreed and wanted to take along John Mark. Paul disagreed strongly since John Mark had deserted them in Pamphylia. Their disagreement was so sharp that Barnabas took John Mark with him and sailed for Cyprus while Paul chose Silas and traveled throughout Syria and Cilicia to strengthen the churches there.

Paul and Silas went first to Derbe and then to Lystra. There they met Timothy, a young disciple whose mother was a Jewish believer but whose father was a Greek. Timothy was well thought of by the believers in Lystra and Iconium so Paul wanted him to join them on their journey. In deference to the Jews of the area he arranged for Timothy to be circumcised before they left.[19]

They went from town to town explaining the decision regarding the commandments decided by the apostles and elders in Jerusalem. The churches were strengthened in their faith and grew daily in numbers.

Next Paul and Silas traveled through the area of Phrygia and Galatia because the Holy Spirit had told them

18   From Acts 16-18.
19   Paul was not arguing that Jews shouldn't be circumcised. He was arguing that it was not necessary to be circumcised in order to be saved. Since Timothy was saved, Paul had no problem with allowing Timothy, who was part Jewish, to be circumcised.

not to go into the province of Asia at that time. Coming to the borders of Mysia they headed for the province of Bithynia, but again the Spirit of Jesus did not let them go. Instead, they went on through Mysia to the city of Troas. That night Paul had a vision. He saw a man from Macedonia in northern Greece pleading, "Come over here and help us." We[20] could only conclude that God was calling us to preach the Good News there.

We boarded a boat at Troas and the next day we landed at Neapolis. From there we reached Philippi, a major city of the district of Macedonia and a Roman colony. On the Sabbath we went outside the city to a riverbank. We sat down to speak with some women who had come together.[21] One of them was Lydia from Thyatira, a merchant of expensive purple cloth and a worshiper of God. The Lord opened her heart and she accepted what Paul was saying. She was baptized along with other members of her household and she asked us to be her guests.

One day as we were going down to the place of prayer we met a demon-possessed slave girl, a fortune-teller who earned a lot of money for her masters. She followed along behind us shouting, "These men are servants of the Most High God and they have come to tell you how to be saved." This went on day after day until Paul got so exasperated that he turned and spoke to the demon within her, "I command

20   Note that all of a sudden the narrator changes from third person to first person, "we." This is a strong indication that the writer of the Book of Acts began traveling with Paul from this point on. In their endless skepticism, critics will say that these "we sections" are just a "literary device" to make it look like the writer was a traveling companion of Paul, to give more credibility to the writing. But if the author was just trying to gain more credibility for his writing, why not just write himself back in at the beginning when Jesus ascended or when Peter preached at Pentecost, or when the Jerusalem Council met, etc.?

21 Jewish law required that there be 10 men to form a synagogue. It may be that in this Roman colony of Philippi there weren't enough Jewish men to form a synagogue, which is why the women were meeting down by the river and not in a synagogue on the Sabbath.

you in the name of Jesus Christ to come out of her." Instantly it left her.

Her masters' hopes of wealth were now shattered so they grabbed Paul and Silas and dragged them before the authorities at the marketplace. "The whole city is in an uproar because of these Jews!" they shouted. "They are teaching the people to do things that are against Roman customs."

A mob quickly formed against Paul and Silas, and the city officials ordered them stripped and beaten with wooden rods. They were severely beaten and thrown into prison. The jailer put them into the inner dungeon and clamped their feet in the stocks.

Around midnight, Paul and Silas were praying and singing hymns to God, and the other prisoners were listening. Suddenly, there was a great earthquake, the prison was shaken, the doors flew open and the chains of every prisoner fell off! The jailer woke up to see the prison doors wide open, assumed that the prisoners had escaped, and drew his sword To kill himself. Paul shouted to him, "Don't do it! We are all here!"

Trembling with fear, the jailer called for lights, ran to the dungeon, fell down before Paul and Silas and asked, "Sirs, what must I do to be saved?" They replied, "Believe on the Lord Jesus and you will be saved, along with your entire household." Then they shared the word of the Lord with him and all who lived in his household. The jailer washed their wounds and he, and everyone in his household were baptized. Then he brought them into his house and set a meal before them.

The next morning the city officials sent the police to tell the jailer, "Let those men go!" But Paul replied, "They have publicly beaten us without trial and jailed us, and we are Roman citizens. Now they want us to leave secretly? Certainly not! Let them come themselves to release us!"

The city officials, alarmed to learn that Paul and Silas were Roman citizens, came to the jail and begged them to leave the city. Paul and Silas then returned to the home of Lydia where they met with the believers and encouraged them once more before leaving town.

Paul and Silas traveled to Thessalonica where there was a Jewish synagogue. As was Paul's custom, he went to the synagogue service and for three Sabbaths in a row he interpreted the Scriptures to the people, explaining the prophecies about the sufferings of the Messiah and his rising from the dead.

Some became converts, including many important women of the city, but the Jewish leaders gathered some worthless fellows from the streets to start a riot. They attacked the home of Jason, searching for Paul and Silas. Not finding them there, they dragged Jason and some of the other believers before the city council.

"Paul and Silas have turned the rest of the world upside down and now they are here disturbing our city," they shouted," and Jason let them into his home. They are all guilty of treason against Caesar, for they profess allegiance to another king, Jesus." The people of the city, as well as the city officials, were thrown into turmoil by these reports, but the officials released Jason and the other believers after they had posted bail.

That very night the believers sent Paul and Silas to Berea. When they arrived, they went to the synagogue. The people of Berea were more open-minded than those in Thessalonica and they searched the Scriptures to check up on Paul and Silas, to see if they were really teaching the truth. As a result, many Jews believed as did some of the prominent Greek women and many men.

When some Jews in Thessalonica learned that Paul was preaching the word of God in Berea, they went there and stirred up trouble. The believers acted at once, sending Paul on to the coast while Silas and Timothy remained behind. Those escorting Paul went with him to Athens; [22] then they returned to Berea with a message for Silas and Timothy to join him.

While Paul was waiting for them in Athens he was deeply troubled by all the idols he saw. He went to the synagogue to debate with the Jews and the God-fearing Gentiles and he spoke daily in the public square to all who happened to be there. He also had a debate with some of the Epicurean and Stoic philosophers. When he told them about Jesus and his resurrection they said, "This babbler has picked up some strange ideas." Others said, "He's pushing some foreign religion." They took him to the Council of Philosophers and said "Tell us more about this new religion."

So Paul, standing before the Council, addressed them. When they heard Paul speak of the resurrection of a person who had been dead, some laughed, but others said, "We want to hear more about this later." Some joined him and became believers.

Then Paul left Athens and went to Corinth. There

---

22   Although Athens was not all that large (maybe 10,000?) it was the greatest cultural center of the time. The city was known for its philosophical debate and its abundance of Idols. One Roman writer sarcastically commented that it was easier to find a god in Athens than a man. While in Athens, Paul became greatly concerned about the persecution facing his new church in Thessalonica so he sent Timothy back to encourage and strengthen them. Timothy would later catch up with Paul in Corinth with encouraging news. When Paul moved from Athens to Corinth, he was not moving to the suburbs or some small town. Corinth was one of the great commercial centers of the Roman Empire with a population of several hundred thousand, rivaling Antioch and Alexandria. Corinth had a temple situated on a mountain some 2,000 feet above sea level where at one time hundreds of prostitutes engaged in ritual, religious sex. In fact, Corinth was so well known for its sexual immorality that the name of the city was turned into a verb (korinthiazomai) meaning to practice sexual immorality! It is important to keep this background in mind when reading Paul's letters to the Corinthians below (Stott, 277, 293-296).

he became acquainted with a Jew named Aquila who had recently arrived from Italy with his wife, Priscilla. They had been expelled from Italy as a result of Claudius Caesar's order to deport all Jews from Rome. Paul lived and worked with them for they were tentmakers just as he was.

Each Sabbath found Paul at the synagogue trying to convince the Jews and Greeks alike. After Silas and Timothy came from Macedonia, Paul spent his time preaching to the Jews, telling them, "The Messiah you are looking for is Jesus." When the Jews opposed and insulted him, Paul said, "Your blood be upon your own heads, I am innocent. From now on I will go to the Gentiles."

After that he stayed with Titius Justus, a Gentile who worshiped God and lived next door to the synagogue. Crispus, the leader of the synagogue, and his household believed in the Lord. Many others in Corinth also became believers and were baptized.

One night the Lord spoke to Paul in a vision and told him, "Don't be afraid! Speak out! I am with you and no one will harm you because many people here in this city belong to me." Paul stayed there for the next year and a half, teaching the word of God.

Introduction to First Thessalonians

While Paul was in Corinth, Timothy returned from Thessalonica with great news. Not only were the Thessalonian Christians holding up well, they were thriving, even under persecution! Paul wrote First Thessalonians from Corinth in AD 50, to express his joy at this news, to offer further encouragement, and to answer some of their questions. The essence of First Thessalonians follows:

From Paul and Silvanus and Timothy, to the church of the Thessalonians. Grace and peace to you! We thank God for you constantly in our prayers because we recall your work of faith, love and endurance in our Lord Jesus Christ. Our gospel did not come to you merely in words, but in power and in the Holy Spirit.

You became imitators of us and of the Lord when you received the message that comes from the Holy Spirit, despite great affliction. As a result you became an example to the believers in Macedonia and in Achaia. People everywhere report how you welcomed us and how you turned to God from idols to serve the true God and to wait for his Son from heaven, whom he raised from the dead, Jesus our deliverer from the coming wrath.

Although we were mistreated in Philippi, as you know, we had the courage in our God to declare to you the gospel in spite of much opposition. We never appeared with flattering speech, as you know, nor with a pretext for greed – God is our witness – nor to seek glory from people. Like a nursing mother caring for her own children, we were happy to share with you not only the gospel of God but also our own lives, because you had become dear to us.

By working night and day so as not to impose a burden on any of you, we preached to you the gospel of God. You are witnesses as to how blameless our conduct was toward you. As you know, we treated each one of you as a father treats his own children, exhorting, encouraging and insisting that you live in a way worthy of God.

We thank God that when you received God's message that you heard from us, you accepted it not as a human message, but as it truly is, God's message. You became imitators of God's churches that are in Judea, because you suffered the same things from your countrymen as they did from the Jews, who killed both the Lord Jesus and persecuted us severely. They are displeasing to God because they hinder us from speaking to the Gentiles so that they may be saved.

But when we were separated from you, brothers and

sisters, for a short time we became all the more fervent in our great desire to see you. We wanted to come to you (I, Paul, in fact tried again and again) but Satan thwarted us. When we could bear it no longer, we decided to stay in Athens alone. We sent Timothy, our brother and fellow worker in the gospel of Christ, to strengthen you and encourage you about your faith, so that no one would be shaken by these afflictions. When we were with you, we were telling you in advance that we would suffer affliction, and so it has happened, as you well know. So when I could bear it no longer, I sent to find out about your faith.

Now Timothy has come to us from you and given us the good news of your faith and love and that you long to see us just as we also long to see you! So in all our distress and affliction we were reassured about you through your faith. We pray earnestly to see you. May the Lord cause you to increase in love for one another and for all, so that your hearts are strengthened in holiness to be blameless before our God and Father at the coming of our Lord Jesus with all his saints.

We urge you in the Lord Jesus, that as you received instruction from us about how you must live and please God (as you are in fact living) that you do so more and more. This is God's will: that you become holy, that you keep away from sexual immorality. In this matter no one should violate the rights of his brother, because the Lord is the avenger in all these cases. The one who rejects this is rejecting God, who gives his Holy Spirit to you.

Now you yourselves are taught by God to love one another. Indeed you are practicing it toward the brothers and sisters in all of Macedonia. We urge you to do so more and more, to aspire to lead a quiet life, to attend to your own business, and to work with your hands, as we commanded you. In this way you will live a decent life before outsiders and not be in need.

We do not want you to be uninformed about those who are asleep, so that you will not grieve like the rest who have no hope. We tell you this by the word of the Lord. The Lord himself will come from heaven with the voice of the archangel and with the trumpet of God, and the dead in Christ will rise first. Then we who are alive will be suddenly caught up together with them in the clouds to meet the Lord in the air. And so we will always be with the Lord. Encourage one another with these words.

You know that the day of the Lord will come as a thief in the night. When they are saying, "peace and security," then sudden destruction comes on them, like labor pains, and they will surely not escape. But you are not in the darkness for the day to overtake you like a thief would.

We must stay alert and sober by putting on the breastplate of faith and love and as a helmet our hope for salvation. God did not destine us for wrath but for gaining salvation through our Lord Jesus Christ. He died for us so that whether we are alert or asleep we will come to life together with him. Therefore encourage one another, just as you are in fact doing.

Acknowledge those who preside over you in the Lord. Esteem them most highly in love because of their work. Be at peace among yourselves. Admonish the undisciplined, comfort the discouraged, help the weak, be patient toward all. See that no one pays back evil for evil but always pursue what is good for one another and for all. Always rejoice, constantly pray, in everything give thanks. Do not extinguish the Spirit. Do not treat prophecies with contempt. Examine all things; hold fast to what is good. Stay away from every form of evil.

Now may the God of peace himself make you completely holy and may your spirit and soul and body be kept entirely blameless at the coming of our Lord Jesus Christ. Pray for us. Greet all the brothers and sisters with a holy kiss. Have this letter read to all the brothers and sisters. The grace of our Lord Jesus Christ be with you.

Introduction to Second Thessalonians

Paul's second letter to the Thessalonians, written from Corinth in AD 51, was an attempt to answer questions his first letter raised about the return of Jesus.

From Paul, Silvanus and Timothy, to the church of the Thessalonians. Grace and peace to you from God the Father and the Lord Jesus Christ! We ought to thank God always for you, brothers and sisters, because your faith flourishes more and more.

We boast about you in the churches for your perseverance in all the persecutions you are enduring. It is right for God to repay those who afflict you, and to you who are being afflicted to give rest together with us when the Lord Jesus is revealed from heaven with his mighty angels. With flaming fire he will mete out punishment on those who do not know God and do not obey the gospel of our Lord Jesus. They will undergo the penalty of eternal destruction from the presence of the Lord when he comes.

Now regarding the arrival of our Lord Jesus Christ and our being gathered to be with him, we ask you not to be easily disturbed by any message allegedly from us, to the effect that the day of the Lord is already here. Let no one deceive you. That day will not arrive until the rebellion comes and the man of lawlessness is revealed, the son of destruction. He opposes and exalts himself above every so-called god or object of worship, and as a result he takes his seat in God's temple, displaying himself as God. Surely you recall that I used to tell you these things while I was still with you.

The one who holds him back will do so until he is taken

out of the way, and then the lawless one will be revealed, whom the Lord will destroy by the manifestation of his arrival. The arrival of the lawless one will be by Satan's working with all kinds of miracles, false wonders, and evil deception directed against those who are perishing, because they found no place in their hearts for the truth so as to be saved. Consequently God sends them a deluding influence so that they will believe what is false. All of them who have not believed the truth but have delighted in evil will be condemned.

Therefore, stand firm and hold on to the traditions that we taught you. Pray for us, that the Lord's message may spread quickly and that we may be delivered from perverse and evil people. The Lord is faithful and will strengthen you and protect you from the evil one.

You know yourselves how you must imitate us, because we did not behave without discipline among you, and we did not eat anyone's food without paying. Instead, in toil and drudgery we worked night and day in order not to burden any of you. We used to give you this command: "If anyone is not willing to work, neither should he eat." We hear that some among you are living an undisciplined life, not doing their own work but meddling in the work of others. Now such people we command in the Lord Jesus Christ to work and so provide their own food to eat.

Do not grow weary in doing what is right. If anyone does not obey our message through this letter do not associate closely with him so that he may be ashamed. Yet do not regard him as an enemy, but admonish him as a brother.

Now may the Lord of peace himself give you peace at all times. The Lord be with you all. I, Paul, write this greeting with my own hand, which is how I write in every letter. The grace of our Lord Jesus Christ be with you all.

CHAPTER THREE

Paul's Third Journey [23]

After spending some time in Antioch, Paul went back to Galatia and Phrygia, visiting the believers, encouraging them and helping them to grow in the Lord.

Meanwhile, a Jew named Apollos, an eloquent speaker who knew the Scriptures well, had just arrived in Ephesus[24] from Alexandria in Egypt. When Priscilla and Aquila heard him preaching boldly in the synagogue they took him aside and explained the way of God more accurately. Apollos had been thinking about going to Achaia, and the brothers and sisters in Ephesus encouraged him in this. They wrote to the believers in Achaia asking them to welcome him. When he arrived there, he proved to be of great benefit to those who, by God's grace, had believed. He refuted the Jews with

---

23 From Acts 18-19.

24 Historical Background: In AD 54, while Paul was ministering in Ephesus, Emperor Claudius became deathly ill and died after eating mushrooms. Rumors spread that he had been poisoned by his wife whose character was such that she was not above suspicion. Claudius was succeeded by Nero. At first, this seemed to be a good thing. In his inaugural speech Nero promised reforms to correct the corruption and restore Rome to the golden age of Augustus. In his first few years he was known as generous and merciful. He even lowered taxes. Little did anyone know what was to come! In AD 55 Nero ordered the murder of Britannicus, a famous general and war hero—and Nero's only serious rival. Soon Nero's perverse character began to come out: paranoia, adultery, gross immorality even to the point of incest with his own mother! He and his friends were rumored to prowl the streets at night mugging people, assaulting women and looting shops. While all this was going on, Paul was on his third missionary journey.

powerful arguments in public debate. Using the Scriptures he explained, "The Messiah you are looking for is Jesus."

While Apollos was in Corinth, Paul came to Ephesus where he found several believers and asked, "Did you receive the Holy Spirit when you believed?" "No," they replied, "we don't know what you mean. Paul laid his hands on them, the Holy Spirit came on them, and they spoke in other tongues and prophesied. There were about twelve men in all.

Paul went to the synagogue and preached boldly for the next three months, arguing persuasively about the Kingdom of God. Some rejected his message and publicly spoke against the Way, so Paul left the synagogue and took the believers with him. Then he began preaching daily at the lecture hall of Tyrannus. This went on for the next two years, so that people throughout the province of Asia heard the Lord's message. God gave Paul the power to do unusual miracles so that even when handkerchiefs or cloths that had touched his skin were placed on sick people, they were healed of their diseases and any evil spirits within them came out.

Afterward Paul felt impelled by the Holy Spirit to go over to Macedonia and Achaia before returning to Jerusalem. After that," he said, "I must go on to Rome!" He sent his two ssistants, Timothy and Erastus, on ahead to Macedonia[25] while he stayed awhile longer in the province of Asia.

25 Although Jesus ministered primarily to small villages, Paul focused on the major urban areas. Paul's ministry in Macedonia had focused on its three main cities, Philippi, Berea, and Thessalonica (the capital). When Paul went to the province of Achaia, he ministered briefly in Athens before going on to the capital which was Corinth. When came to Ephesus, he was once again ministering in a major commercial center, the capital of the province of Asia. Ephesus was the site of the Temple of Artimus (or Diana), one of the seven wonders of the ancient world. With over 100 huge pillars reaching 60 feet in the air, this temple was four times the size of the famous Parthenon in Athens. It was a major source of pride and revenue for the city—and a major obstacle for Paul. Paul came to Ephesus and as was his custom, he began ministering in the synagogue (Stott, 294).

Introduction to First Corinthians

In AD 55 a group of believers from the Church in Corinth traveled to meet Paul in Ephesus with a letter and with disturbing news about divisions in the church. Paul responded by writing the letter that we now know as "First Corinthians." In this letter Paul addresses the problem of division in their church and then answers questions from the letter sent to him by the Corinthians, questions about sexuality, marriage, worship, the resurrection of Jesus and giving. Paul intended to visit the Corinthians personally but in the mean time he sent Timothy to drop off the letter in Corinth on his (Timothy's) way to Macedonia. The essence of this letter is below:

From Paul, an apostle of Christ Jesus and Sosthenes our brother, to the church in Corinth. Grace and peace to you from God our Father and the Lord Jesus Christ!

I thank God for you because of the grace of God that was given to you in Christ Jesus. You were made rich in every way in him – so that you do not lack any spiritual gift. God is faithful, by whom you were called into fellowship with his son, Jesus Christ our Lord.

I urge you, brothers and sisters, by the name of our Lord Jesus Christ, to end your divisions. Members of Chloe's household have made it clear to me that there are quarrels among you, that each of you is saying, "I am with Paul," or "I am with Apollos," or "I am with Cephas," or "I am with Christ." Is Christ divided? Paul wasn't crucified for you, was he? Were you baptized in the name of Paul?

The message about the cross is foolishness to those who are perishing, but to us who are being saved it is the power of God. Since the world by its wisdom did not know God, God was pleased to save those who believe by the foolishness of preaching. We preach about a crucified Christ, a stumbling block to Jews and foolishness to Gentiles. But to those who are called, both Jews and Greeks, Christ is the power of God and the wisdom of God.

God chose what is low and despised in the world, to set aside what is regarded as something, so that no one can boast in his presence. He is the reason you have a relationship with Christ Jesus, who became for us wisdom from God, and righteousness and sanctification and redemption.

When I came to you, brothers and sisters, I did not come with superior eloquence or wisdom as I proclaimed the testimony of God. I decided to be concerned about nothing among you except Jesus Christ and him crucified. I was with you in fear and with much trembling. My conversation and my preaching were not with persuasive words of wisdom but with a demonstration of the Spirit and of power, so that your faith would not be based on human wisdom but on the power of God.

We speak the wisdom of God hidden in a mystery that God determined before the ages. None of the rulers of this age understood it. If they had known it, they would not have crucified the Lord of glory. As it is written, "**Things that no eye has seen, or ear heard, or mind imagined are the things God has prepared for those who love him.**" God has revealed these to us by the Spirit. The unbeliever does not receive the things of the Spirit of God because they are spiritually discerned.

Brothers and sisters, I could not speak to you as spiritual people but instead as people of the flesh, as infants in Christ. I fed you milk, not solid food, for you were not yet ready. You are still not ready since there is still jealousy and dissension among you. Are you not behaving like unregenerate people? Someone says, "I am with Paul," or "I am with Apollos." What is Apollos or what is Paul? Servants through whom you came to believe!

I planted, Apollos watered, but God caused it to grow.

Neither the one who plants counts for anything, nor the one who waters, but God who causes the growth. The one who plants and the one who waters work as one, but each will receive his reward according to his work. We are coworkers belonging to God. You are God's field, God's building.

According to the grace of God given to me, like a skilled master-builder I laid a foundation but someone else builds on it. No one can lay any foundation other than Jesus Christ. If anyone builds on the foundation with gold, silver, precious stones, wood, hay, or straw, each builder's work will be plainly seen, for the Day will make it clear, because it will be revealed by fire. The fire will test what kind of work each has done. If what someone has built survives, he will receive a reward. If someone's work is burned up, he will suffer loss. He himself will be saved, but only as through fire.

Do you not know that you are God's temple and that God's Spirit lives in you? If someone destroys God's temple, God will destroy him. God's temple is holy, which is what you are. Guard against self-deception. The wisdom of this age is foolishness with God.

Think about us as servants of Christ and stewards of the mysteries of God. What is sought in stewards is that one be found faithful. So for me, it is a minor matter that I am judged by you or by any human court. In fact, I do not even judge myself. I am not aware of anything against myself but I am not acquitted because of this. The one who judges me is the Lord. Do not judge anything before the time. Wait until the Lord comes. He will bring to light the hidden things of darkness and reveal the motives of hearts. Then each will receive recognition from God.

I have applied these things to myself and Apollos so that none of you will be puffed up in favor of the one against the other. God has exhibited us apostles as men condemned to die because we have become a spectacle to the world. To the present hour we are hungry and thirsty, poorly clothed, brutally treated, and without a roof over our heads. We do hard work, toiling with our own hands. When we are verbally abused, we respond with a blessing, when persecuted, we endure, when people lie about us, we answer in a friendly manner

.I am not writing these things to shame you, but to correct you as my dear children. Though you may have ten thousand guardians in Christ, you do not have many fathers. I became your father in Christ Jesus through the gospel. I encourage you, then, be imitators of me.

I have sent Timothy to you, my dear and faithful son in the Lord. He will remind you of my ways in Christ. Some have become arrogant, as if I were not coming to you. But I will come to you soon, if the Lord is willing, and I will find out not only the talk of these arrogant people, but also their power. Shall I come to you with a rod of discipline or with love and a spirit of gentleness?

It is actually reported that sexual immorality exists among you, the kind of immorality that is not permitted even among the Gentiles, that someone is cohabiting with his father's wife. Shouldn't you have been deeply sorrowful and removed the one who did this from among you? I have already judged the one who did this. When you gather together in the name of our Lord Jesus turn this man over to Satan for the destruction of the flesh so that his spirit may be saved in the day of the Lord. Don't you know that a little yeast affects the whole batch of dough? Christ, our Passover lamb has been sacrificed. Let us celebrate the festival, not with the old yeast of vice and evil, but with the bread without yeast, the bread of sincerity and truth.

I wrote you in my letter not to associate with sexually immoral people. In no way did I mean the immoral people of this world, or the greedy and swindlers and idolaters, since you would then have to go out of the world. But now I am writing to you not to associate with anyone who calls himself a Christian who is sexually immoral, or greedy, or an idolater, or verbally abusive, or a drunkard, or a swindler. Do not even eat with such a person. Remove the evil person from among you.

When any of you has a legal dispute with another, does he dare go to court before the unrighteous rather than before the saints? Do you not know that the saints will judge the world? Is there no one among you wise enough to settle disputes between fellow Christians? Instead, does a Christian sue a Christian, and do this before unbelievers? Why not rather be wronged? But you yourselves wrong and cheat, and you do this to your brothers and sisters!

Do you not know that the unrighteous will not inherit the kingdom of God? Do not be deceived! The sexually immoral, idolaters, adulterers, practicing homosexuals, thieves, the greedy, drunkards, the verbally abusive, and swindlers will not inherit the kingdom of God. Some of you once lived this way but you were washed, sanctified, you were justified in the name of the Lord Jesus Christ and by the Spirit of our God.

The body is not for sexual immorality, but for the Lord. Do you not know that your bodies are members of Christ? Should I take the members of Christ and make them members of a prostitute? Never! Flee sexual immorality! Your body is the temple of the Holy Spirit who is in you and you are not your own. You were bought at a price therefore glorify God with your body.

Now with regard to the issues you wrote about: It is good for a man not to have sexual relations with a woman, but because of immoralities, each man should have relations with his own wife and each woman with her own husband. Do not deprive each other, except by mutual agreement for a specified time, so that you may devote yourselves to prayer. Then resume your relationship, so that Satan may not tempt you because of your lack of self-control.

To the unmarried and widows I say that it is best for them to remain as I am. But if they do not have self-control, let them get married. For it is better to marry than to burn with sexual desire.

To the married I give this command – not I, but the Lord – a wife should not divorce a husband (but if she does, let her remain unmarried, or be reconciled to her husband), and a husband should not divorce his wife.

To the rest I say – I, not the Lord – if a brother has a wife who is not a believer and she is happy to live with him, he should not divorce her. If a woman has a husband who is not a believer and he is happy to live with her, she should not divorce him. If the unbeliever wants a divorce, let it take place. In these circumstances the brother or sister is not bound. How do you know, wife, whether you will bring your husband to salvation? Or how do you know, husband, whether you will bring your wife to salvation?

With regard to the question about people who have never married, I have no command from the Lord, but I give my opinion as one shown mercy by the Lord to be trustworthy. Because of the impending crisis I think it best for you to remain as you are. The one bound to a wife should not seek divorce. The one released from a wife should not seek marriage. But if you marry, you have not sinned. Those who marry will face difficult circumstances, and I am trying to spare you such problems.

I want you to be free from concern. An unmarried man is concerned about how to please the Lord but a married man is concerned about how to please his wife, and he is divided. An unmarried woman is concerned about the things of the Lord but a married woman is concerned about how to please her husband. I am saying this so that without distraction you may give notable and constant service to the Lord.

A wife is bound as long as her husband is living. If her husband dies she is free to marry anyone she wishes (only someone in the Lord). In my opinion, she will be happier if she remains as she is – and I think that I too have the Spirit of God!

With regard to eating food sacrificed to idols, we know that "an idol is nothing," and that "there is no God but one." There is one God, the Father, from whom are all things and for whom we live, and one Lord, Jesus Christ, through whom are all things and through whom we live.

But some, by being accustomed to idols in former times, eat this food as an idol sacrifice, and their conscience, because it is weak, is defiled. We are no worse if we do not eat and no better if we do. But be careful that this liberty does not become a hindrance to the weak. If someone weak sees you dining in an idol's temple, will not his conscience be "strengthened" to eat food offered to idols? If you sin against your brothers or sisters in this way and wound their weak conscience, you sin against Christ. If food causes my brother or sister to sin, I will never eat meat again, so that I may not cause one of them to sin.

Am I not an apostle? Have I not seen Jesus our Lord? Do we not have the right to financial support? Do we not have the right to the company of a believing wife, like the other apostles and the Lord's brothers and Cephas? But we have not made use of this right. Instead we endure everything so that we may not be a hindrance to the gospel of Christ.

Don't you know that those who serve in the temple eat food from the temple? In the same way the Lord commanded those who proclaim the gospel to receive their living by the gospel. But I have not used any of these rights and I am not writing so something will be done for me. No one will deprive me of my reason for boasting! For if I preach the gospel, I have no reason for boasting, because I am compelled to do this. Woe to me if I do not preach the gospel!

To the Jews I became like a Jew to gain the Jews. To those free from the law I became like one free from the law (though I am not free from God's law but under the law of Christ) to gain those free from the law. To the weak I became weak in order to gain the weak. I have become all things to all people, so that by all means I may save some.

All the runners in a stadium compete but only one receives the prize. So run to win. Each competitor must exercise self-control in everything. They do it to receive a perishable crown, but we an imperishable one. I do not run uncertainly or box like one who hits only air. I subdue my body and make it my slave, so that after preaching to others I myself will not be disqualified.

I do not want you to be unaware, brothers and sisters that our fathers all passed through the sea and were baptized into Moses. But God was not pleased with most of them for they were cut down in the wilderness. These things happened as examples for us. Do not be idolaters, as some of them were. Let us not be immoral, as some of them were, and twenty-three thousand died in a single day. Let us not put Christ to the test, as some of them did and were destroyed by snakes. Do not complain, as some of them did and were killed by the destroying angel. These things were written for our instruction.

Let the one who thinks he is standing be careful that he does not fall. No trial has overtaken you that is not faced by others. God is faithful: He will not let you be tried beyond what you are able to bear but with the trial will also provide a way out so that you may be able to endure it.

Flee from idolatry. Is not the cup of blessing that we bless a sharing in the blood of Christ? Is not the bread that we break a sharing in the body of Christ? What the pagans sacrifice is to demons and not to God. You cannot take part in the table of the Lord and the table of demons.

Do not seek your own good, but the good of the other person. Eat anything that is sold in the marketplace without questions of conscience. If an unbeliever invites you to dinner, eat whatever is served without asking questions of conscience. But if someone says to you, "This is from a sacrifice," do not eat, because of conscience –not yours but the other person's. Whether you eat or drink, or whatever you do, do everything for the glory of God. Do not give offense to Jews or Greeks or to the church of God. I do not seek my own benefit, but the benefit of many, so that they may be saved. Be imitators of me, just as I also am of Christ.

I want you to know that Christ is the head of every man, the man is the head of a woman, and God is the head of Christ. Any man who prays or prophesies with his head covered disgraces his head. Any woman who prays or prophesies with her head uncovered disgraces her head.

Now when you come together as a church you are not really eating the Lord's Supper, for when it is time to eat, everyone proceeds with his own supper. One is hungry and another becomes drunk. Do you not have houses so that you can eat and drink? Or are you trying to show contempt for the church of God by shaming those who have nothing?

I received from the Lord what I also passed on to you, that the Lord Jesus on the night in which he was betrayed took bread, and after he had given thanks he broke it and said, "This is my body, which is for you. Do this in remembrance of me." In the same way, he also took the cup after supper, saying, "This cup is the new covenant in my blood. Do this, every time you drink it, in remembrance of me." For every time you eat this bread and drink the cup, you proclaim the Lord's death until he comes.

Whoever eats the bread or drinks the cup of the Lord in an unworthy manner will be guilty of the body and blood of the Lord. A person should examine himself first. The one who eats and drinks without careful regard for the body eats and drinks judgment against himself. That is why many of you are weak and sick, and quite a few are dead. But if we examined ourselves, we would not be judged. When you come together to eat, wait for one another. If anyone is hungry, let him eat at home, so that when you assemble it does not lead to judgment.

With regard to spiritual gifts, brothers and sisters: There are different gifts, but the same Spirit. There are different ministries, but the same Lord. To each person the manifestation of the Spirit is given for the benefit of all. One person is given the message of wisdom, and another the message of knowledge, to another faith, and to another gifts of healing, to another performance of miracles, to another prophecy, to another discernment of spirits, to another different kinds of tongues, and to another the interpretation of tongues. It is one and the same Spirit, distributing as he decides to each person, who produces all these things.

Just as the body is one and yet has many members, so too is Christ. In one Spirit we were all baptized into one body, whether Jews or Greeks or slaves or free. If the whole body were an eye, what part would do the hearing? If the whole were an ear, what part would exercise the sense of smell? God has placed each of the members in the body just as he decided. The eye cannot say to the hand, "I do not need you," nor can the head say to the foot, "I do not need you." On the contrary, those members that seem to be weaker are essential. God has blended together the body, giving greater honor to the lesser member, so that there may be no division in the body, but the members may have mutual concern for one another. If one member suffers, everyone suffers. If a member is honored, all rejoice.

You are Christ's body and each of you is a member of it. God has placed in the church first apostles, second prophets, third teachers, then miracles, gifts of healing, helps, gifts of leadership, different kinds of tongues. Not all are apostles, are they? Not all are prophets, are they? Not all are teachers, are they? Not all perform miracles, do they? Not all have gifts of healing, do they? Not all speak in tongues, do they? Not all interpret, do they? But you should be eager for the greater gifts.

Now I will show you a way that is beyond comparison. If I speak in the tongues of men and of angels but I do not have love, I am a noisy gong or a clanging cymbal. If I have prophecy, know all mysteries and all knowledge, and if I have all faith so that I can remove mountains, but do not have love, I am nothing. If I give away everything I own but do not have love, I receive no benefit.

Love is patient, kind, not envious, does not brag, is not puffed up, is not rude, is not self-serving, is not easily angered or resentful. It is not glad about injustice, but rejoices in the truth. It bears all things, believes all things, hopes all things, endures all things.

Love never ends. Prophecies will be set aside; Tongues will cease; Knowledge will be set aside. We know in part and we prophesy in part, but when what is perfect comes, the partial will be set aside. When I was a child, I talked like a child, I thought like a child, I reasoned like a child. When I became an adult, I set aside childish ways. Now we see in a mirror indirectly but then we will see face to face. Now I know in part but then I will know fully. Now these three remain: faith, hope, and love, but the greatest of these is love.

Pursue love and be eager for the spiritual gifts, especially that you may prophesy. The one speaking in a tongue does not speak to people but to God, for no one understands. The one who prophesies speaks to people for their strengthening, encouragement, and consolation. The one who speaks in a tongue builds himself up, but the one who prophesies builds up the church. I wish you all spoke in tongues, but even more that you would prophesy. The one who prophesies is greater than the one who speaks in tongues, unless he interprets so that the church may be strengthened.

If I come to you speaking in tongues, how will I help you

unless I speak to you with a revelation or with knowledge or prophecy or teaching? Since you are eager for manifestations of the Spirit, seek to abound in order to strengthen the church.

So then, one who speaks in a tongue should pray that he may interpret. If I pray in a tongue, my spirit prays, but my mind is unproductive. What should I do? I will pray with my spirit, but I will also pray with my mind. I will sing praises with my spirit, but I will also sing praises with my mind. Otherwise, if you are praising God with your spirit, how can someone without the gift say "Amen" to your thanksgiving, since he does not know what you are saying? I thank God that I speak in tongues more than all of you, but in the church I want to speak five words with my mind to instruct others, rather than ten thousand words in a tongue.

Tongues are a sign for unbelievers. Prophecy, however, is for believers. If the whole church comes together and all speak in tongues, and unbelievers or uninformed people enter, will they not say that you have lost your minds? But if all prophesy and an unbeliever or uninformed person enters, he will be convicted by all.

When you come together, let all these things be done for the strengthening of the church. If someone speaks in a tongue, it should be two, or at the most three, one after the other, and someone must interpret. If there is no interpreter, he should be silent in the church. Two or three prophets should speak and the others should evaluate what is said. If someone receives a revelation, the person who is speaking should conclude. You can all prophesy one after another, so all can learn and be encouraged. Indeed, the spirits of the prophets are subject to the prophets, for God is not characterized by disorder but by peace.

Women should be silent in the churches for they are not permitted to speak. Rather, let them be in submission, as in fact the law says. If they want to find out about something, they should ask their husbands at home, because it is disgraceful for a woman to speak in church.

If anyone considers himself a prophet or spiritual person he should acknowledge that what I write to you is the Lord's command. So then, brothers and sisters, be eager to prophesy and do not forbid anyone from speaking in tongues. Do everything in a decent and orderly manner.

Now I want to make clear for you the gospel by which you are being saved if you hold firmly to the message I preached. I passed on to you as of first importance what I also received – that Christ died for our sins, was buried, and was raised on the third day according to the scriptures, and that he appeared to Cephas, then to the twelve.

Then he appeared to more than five hundred of the brothers and sisters at one time, most of whom are still alive, though some have fallen asleep. Then he appeared to James, then to all the apostles. Last of all he appeared to me also, for I am the least of the apostles, unworthy to be called an apostle, because I persecuted the church of God. But by the grace of God I am what I am.

Now how can some of you say there is no resurrection of the dead? If there is no resurrection of the dead, then not even Christ has been raised. And if Christ has not been raised, then our preaching is futile and your faith is empty. Also, we are found to be false witnesses about God, because we have testified that he raised Christ from the dead. And if Christ has not been raised, your faith is useless; you are still in your sins. Furthermore, those who have fallen asleep in Christ have also perished.

But Christ has been raised from the dead! Just as in Adam all die, so also in Christ all will be made alive. He must reign until he has put all his enemies under his feet. The last enemy to be eliminated is death. When all things are subjected to him, then the Son himself will be subjected to the one who subjected everything to him, so that God may be *all in all. If the dead are not raised, let us eat and drink, for tomorrow we die. Do not be deceived: "Bad company corrupts good morals." Sober up and stop sinning!*

But someone will say, "How are the dead raised? With what kind of body will they come?" Fool! What you sow will not come to life unless it dies, and what you sow is not the body that is to be, but a bare seed. But God gives it a body just as he planned. It is the same with the resurrection of the dead. What is sown is perishable, what is raised is imperishable. It is sown a natural body, it is raised a spiritual body.

Flesh and blood cannot inherit the kingdom of God nor does the perishable inherit the imperishable. I will tell you a mystery: We will not all sleep, but we will all be changed – in a moment, in the blinking of an eye, at the last trumpet. For the trumpet will sound and the dead will be raised imperishable. This perishable body must put on the imperishable and this mortal body must put on immortality. So then, dear brothers and sisters, be firm. Do not be moved! Always be outstanding in the work of the Lord knowing that your labor is not in vain in the Lord.

With regard to the collection for the saints, please follow the directions that I gave to the churches of Galatia: On the first day of the week, each of you should set aside some income and save it to the extent that God has blessed you, so that a collection will not have to be made when I come. Then, when I arrive, I will send those whom you approve to carry your gift to Jerusalem. If it seems advisable that I should go also, they will go with me.

I will come to you after I have gone through Macedonia and perhaps I will stay with you, or even spend the winter. With regard to our brother Apollos: I strongly encouraged him to visit you with the other brothers but it was simply not his intention to come now. He will come when he has the opportunity. Stay alert, stand firm in the faith, show courage, be strong. Everything you do should be done in love.

I was glad about the arrival of Stephanus, Fortunatus, and Achaicus because they have supplied the fellowship with you that I lacked. The churches in the province of Asia send greetings to you. Aquila and Prisca greet you warmly in the Lord, with the church that meets in their house. All the brothers and sisters send greetings. Greet one another with a holy kiss.

I, Paul, send this greeting with my own hand. Let anyone who has no love for the Lord be accursed. Our Lord, come! The grace of the Lord Jesus be with you. My love be with all of you in Christ Jesus.

CHAPTER FOUR

Paul's Third Journey: Second Corinthians

Introduction to the "Harsh Letter"

After writing First Corinthians, Paul later followed up by making a personal visit to Corinth as he had planned. Unfortunately, there was a faction in the Corinthian church that didn't appreciate Paul's ministry and was apparently turning the church against him. The resulting confrontation was not pleasant and Paul later characterized his visit as "painful."[1] Paul left Corinth not exactly on the best terms. In fact, when he got to Macedonia he sent his colleague Titus back to Corinth with another letter to the Corinthians which was apparently a bit harsh, causing the Corinthians to "grieve."[2] Unfortunately, this letter has been lost.

There are some scholars, however, who think that the last four chapters of Second Corinthians (chapters 10-13) are actually part of the "harsh" letter and that it was added to Second Corinthians by some scribe at a later date. There is absolutely no external evidence for this theory. In other words, no ancient manuscripts of Second Corinthians have ever been discovered in which chapters 10-13 are missing and there are no manuscripts indicating that 10-13 were once a separate letter.

But while there is no external evidence that Second Corinthians 10-13 was the harsh letter, the essence of those chapters has been placed out of order below strictly for educational purposes, because they give a good idea of what a harsh letter from Paul might have sounded like.

Now I, Paul, appeal to you personally (I who am meek when present among you, but am full of courage toward you when away)![26] We do not wage war according to human standards, for the weapons of our warfare are not human weapons, but are made powerful by God for tearing arguments and every arrogant obstacle that is raised up against the knowledge of God. We take every thought captive to make it obey Christ.

I do not want to seem as though I am trying to terrify you with my letters, because some say, "His letters are weighty and forceful, but his physical presence is weak and his speech is of no account." What we say by letters when we are absent, we also are in actions when we are present.

We would not dare to compare ourselves with some of those who recommend themselves. We will confine our boasting according to the limits of the work to which God has appointed us. We hope that as your faith continues to grow our work may be greatly expanded among you so that we may preach the gospel in the regions that lie beyond you, and not boast of work already done in another person's area.

If someone comes and proclaims another Jesus different from the one we proclaimed or a different gospel than the one you accepted, you put up with it well enough! I consider myself not at all inferior to those "super-apostles." Even if I am unskilled in speaking, I am certainly not so in knowledge.

Did I commit a sin by humbling myself, because I proclaimed the gospel of God to you free of charge? When I was with you and was in need I was not a burden to anyone, for the brothers who came from Macedonia fully supplied my needs. I kept myself from being a burden to you in any way, and will continue to do so.

---

26   In this parenthetical phrase, Paul is probably quoting what his opponents are saying about him.

What I am doing I will continue to do, so that I may eliminate any opportunity for those who want to be regarded as our equals in the things they boast about. Such people are false apostles, deceitful workers, disguising themselves as apostles of Christ. No wonder, for even Satan disguises himself as an angel of light. Therefore it is not surprising his servants also disguise themselves as servants of righteousness.

Since many are boasting according to human standards, I too will boast (I am speaking foolishly).

Are they Hebrews? So am I.

Are they Israelites? So am I.

Are they descendants of Abraham? So am I.

Are they servants of Christ? (I am talking like I am out of my mind!) I am even more so: with much greater labors, with far more imprisonments, with more severe beatings, facing death many times. Five times I received from the Jews forty lashes less one. Three times I was beaten with a rod. Once I received a stoning. Three times I suffered shipwreck. A night and a day I spent adrift in the open sea. I have been on journeys many times, in dangers from rivers, from robbers, from my own countrymen, from Gentiles, in dangers in the city, in the wilderness, at sea, in dangers from false brothers, in hard work and toil, through many sleepless nights, in hunger and thirst, many times without food, in cold and without enough clothing. Apart from other things, there is the daily pressure on me of my anxious concern for all the churches.

If I must boast, I will boast about the things that show my weakness. The God and Father of the Lord Jesus knows I am not lying. In Damascus, the governor under King Aretas was guarding the city of Damascus in order to arrest me but I was let down in a rope-basket through a window in the city wall, and escaped his hands.

I will go on to visions and revelations from the Lord.

I know a man in Christ who fourteen years ago (whether in the body or out of the body I do not know, God knows) was caught up to the third heaven. This man (whether in the body or apart from the body I do not know, God knows) was caught up into paradise and heard things too sacred to be put into words, things that a person is not permitted to speak.

On behalf of such an individual I will boast, but on my own behalf I will not boast, except about my weaknesses. Even if I wish to boast, I would be telling the truth, but I refrain from this so that no one may regard me beyond what he sees in me or what he hears from me, even because of the extraordinary character of the revelations.

Therefore, a thorn in the flesh was given to me, a messenger of Satan to trouble me so that I would not become arrogant. I asked the Lord three times about this, that it would depart from me. He said to me, "My grace is enough for you, for my power is made perfect in weakness." So then, I will boast most gladly about my weaknesses, so that the power of Christ may reside in me. Therefore I am content with weaknesses, with insults, with troubles, with persecutions and difficulties for the sake of Christ, for whenever I am weak, then I am strong.

I lack nothing in comparison to those "super-apostles," even though I am nothing. Indeed, the signs of an apostle were performed among you with great perseverance by signs and wonders and powerful deeds.

For the third time I am ready to come to you. I will not be a burden to you because I do not want your possessions, but you. If I love you more, am I to be loved less? But be that as it may, I have not burdened you. I have not taken advantage of you through anyone I have sent to you, have I? I urged Titus to visit you and I sent our brother along with him. Titus did not take advantage of you, did he? Everything we do, dear friends, is to build you up.

I am afraid that there may be quarreling, jealousy,

intense anger, selfish ambition, slander, gossip, arrogance, and disorder. I am afraid that God may humiliate me before you, and I will grieve for many of those who previously sinned and have not repented of the impurity, sexual immorality, and licentiousness that they have practiced.

This is the third time I am coming to visit you. I said before when I was present the second time and now I say again that if I come again I will not spare anyone since you are demanding proof that Christ is speaking through me. Indeed he was crucified by reason of weakness but he lives because of God's power. We also are weak in him but we will live together with him, because of God's power toward you.

Put yourselves to the test to see if you are in the faith; examine yourselves! Do you not recognize regarding yourselves that Jesus Christ is in you – unless, indeed, you fail the test! I am writing these things while absent, so that when I arrive I may not have to deal harshly with you by using my authority – the Lord gave it to me for building up, not for tearing down!

Finally, brothers and sisters, rejoice, set things right, be encouraged, agree with one another, live in peace, and the God of love and peace will be with you. Greet one another with a holy kiss. All the saints greet you. The grace of the Lord Jesus Christ and the love of God and the fellowship of the Holy Spirit be with you all.

Paul's Third Missionary Journey continued[3]

Paul wrote his "harsh" letter to the Corinthians from somewhere in Macedonia. He sent Titus to deliver the letter and Paul apparently continued his ministry. Although Paul had told the Corinthians he was coming right back to them, he changed his mind, not wanting to cause the Corinthians further pain, and apparently returned to Ephesus where the danger intensified.

About that time, serious trouble developed in Ephesus concerning "the Way."[27] It began with Demetrius, a silversmith who had a large business manufacturing silver shrines of the Greek goddess Artemis. He called the craftsmen together, along with others employed in related trades, and addressed them:

Gentlemen, you know that our wealth comes from this business. As you have seen and heard, this man Paul has persuaded many people that handmade gods aren't gods at all. Of course, I'm not just talking about the loss of public respect for our business. I'm also concerned that the temple of the great goddess Artemis will be robbed of her prestige!

At this their anger boiled and they began shouting, "Great is Artemis of the Ephesians!" A crowd began to gather and soon the city was filled with confusion. Everyone rushed to the amphitheater, dragging along Gaius and Aristarchus who were Paul's traveling companions from Macedonia. Paul wanted to go in but the believers wouldn't let him. Some of the officials of the province, friends of Paul, also sent a message to him, begging him not to risk his life by entering the amphitheater.

At last the mayor was able to quiet them down enough to speak. "Citizens of Ephesus," he said   "Everyone knows that Ephesus is the official guardian of the temple of the great Artemis, whose image fell down to us from heaven. Since this is an indisputable fact, you shouldn't be disturbed no matter what is said. Don't do anything rash. I am afraid we are in danger of being charged with rioting by the Roman government. If Rome demands an explanation we won't know what to say."

Then he dismissed them and they dispersed. When it was all over Paul sent for the believers and encouraged them. Then he left for Macedonia. Along the way he encouraged the believers in all the towns he passed through

---

27   "The Way" was one of the earliest names for Christianity.

Introduction to Second Corinthians

After the riot, Paul left Ephesus for Macedonia. He had apparently planned to meet Titus (whom he had sent to deliver his "harsh letter" to Corinth) in Troas but when Paul got to Troas, Titus didn't show up. In the following letter, Paul says that even though God opened a door for him to preach the Gospel in Troas, he was so concerned about his friend Titus he went on to Macedonia looking for him.

In Macedonia, Paul found Titus, who was not only alive and well, but had great news that the Corinthians had responded well to Paul's "harsh" letter. They had repented and were eagerly looking forward to seeing Paul again. Paul was so overjoyed, that in AD 56 he wrote the letter we know as Second Corinthians to the church in Corinth from somewhere in Macedonia. His purpose was to express his joy, to pour out his heart, to explain why he had not come back when he told them he would, and to ask them to prepare for his next visit. The essence of Second Corinthians 1-9 appears below.

From Paul, an apostle of Christ Jesus by the will of God, and Timothy our brother, to the church that is in Corinth. Grace and peace to you from God our Father and the Lord Jesus Christ!

Blessed is the God and Father of our Lord Jesus Christ who comforts us in all our troubles so that we may be able to comfort those experiencing any trouble. We know that as you share in our sufferings, so also you will share in our comfort.

We do not want you to be unaware, brothers and sisters, regarding the affliction that happened to us in the province of Asia, that we were burdened excessively, beyond our strength, so that we despaired even of living.

We felt as if the sentence of death had been passed against us, so that we would not trust in ourselves but in God who raises the dead. He delivered us from so great a risk of death. We have set our hope on him that he will deliver us yet again, as you also join in helping us by prayer, so that many people may give thanks to God on our behalf.

Our reason for confidence is this: that with pure motives and sincerity which are from God we conducted ourselves in the world and toward you. With this confidence I intended to come to you and to go on into Macedonia and then from Macedonia to come back to you and be helped on our way into Judea by you.

Now I appeal to God as my witness, that to spare you I did not come again to Corinth. I made up my mind not to pay you another painful visit, and I wrote to you so that when I came I would not have sadness from those who ought to make me rejoice. Out of great distress and anguish of heart I wrote to you with many tears, not to make you sad, but to let you know the love that I have especially for you.

If anyone has caused sadness, he has not saddened me alone, but to some extent he has saddened all of you as well. This punishment on such an individual by the majority is enough for him, so now you should forgive and comfort him. This will keep him from being overwhelmed by excessive grief to the point of despair. Therefore I urge you to reaffirm your love for him. If you forgive anyone for anything, I also forgive him.

Now when I arrived in Troas to proclaim the gospel of Christ, even though the Lord had opened a door of opportunity for me, I had no relief in my spirit because I did not find my brother Titus there. So I set out for Macedonia.

We are not like so many others, hucksters who peddle the word of God for profit. We are speaking in Christ before

God as persons of sincerity sent from God.

We don't need letters of recommendation to you or from you as some other people do, do we? You yourselves are our letter, written on our hearts, written not with ink but by the Spirit of the living God, not on stone tablets but on tablets of human hearts.

We have confidence in God through Christ. Our adequacy is from God, who made us adequate to be servants of a new covenant not based on the letter but on the Spirit, for the letter kills, but the Spirit gives life. If the ministry that produced death – carved in letters on stone tablets – came with glory, how much more glorious will the ministry of the Spirit be?

Therefore, since we have such a hope, we behave with great boldness, and not like Moses who used to put a veil over his face to keep the Israelites from staring at the result of the glory that was made ineffective. To this very day the same veil remains when they hear the old covenant read, but when one turns to the Lord, the veil is removed.

Therefore, since we have this ministry we do not become discouraged. We have rejected shameful hidden deeds, not behaving with deceptiveness or distorting the word of God. By open proclamation of the truth we commend ourselves to everyone's conscience before God. Even if our gospel is veiled, it is veiled only to those who are perishing. The god of this age has blinded the minds of those who do not believe so they would not see the light of the glorious gospel of Christ, who is the image of God. We do not proclaim ourselves but Jesus Christ as Lord.

We have this treasure in clay jars so that the extraordinary power belongs to God not from us. We are experiencing trouble on every side but are not crushed; we are perplexed, but not driven to despair; we are persecuted but not abandoned; we are knocked down but not destroyed. We are constantly being handed over to death for Jesus' sake so that the life of Jesus may also be made visible in our mortal body.

We know that the one who raised up Jesus will also raise us up with Jesus and will bring us with you into his presence. Therefore we do not despair, but even if our physical body is wearing away, our inner person is being renewed day by day. For our momentary, light suffering is producing for us an eternal weight of glory far beyond all comparison because we are not looking at what can be seen but at what cannot be seen. What can be seen is temporary but what cannot be seen is eternal.

We know that if our earthly house, the tent we live in, is dismantled, we have a building from God, a house not built by human hands, that is eternal in the heavens. In this earthly house we groan, because we desire to put on our heavenly dwelling. Now the one who prepared us for this very purpose is God, who gave us the Spirit as a down payment. Therefore we are always full of courage and would prefer to be away from the body and at home with the Lord. Whether we are alive or away, we make it our ambition to please him. We must all appear before the judgment seat of Christ so that each one may be paid back according to what he has done while in the body, whether good or evil.

Therefore, because we know the fear of the Lord, we try to persuade people. We are not trying to commend ourselves to you again, but are giving you an opportunity to be proud of us so that you may be able to answer those who take pride in outward appearance and not in what is in the heart. For the love of Christ controls us. Christ died for all so that those who live should no longer live for themselves but for him who died for them and was raised. If anyone is in Christ, he is a new creation; what is old has passed away – what is new has come!

All these things are from God who reconciled us to himself through Christ and who has given us the ministry of reconciliation. In other words, in Christ God was reconciling the world to himself, not counting people's trespasses against them, and he has given us the message of reconciliation. Therefore we are ambassadors for Christ, as though God were making His plea through us. We plead with you on Christ's behalf, "Be reconciled to God!" God made the one who did not know sin to be sin for us, so that in him we would become the righteousness of God.

Because we are fellow workers, we also urge you not to receive the grace of God in vain. Now is **the acceptable time**. Now is **the day of salvation!** As God's servants we have commended ourselves in every way, with great endurance, in persecutions, in difficulties, in distresses, in beatings, in imprisonments, in riots, in troubles, in sleepless nights, in hunger, by purity, by knowledge, by patience, by benevolence, by the Holy Spirit, by genuine love, by truthful teaching, by the power of God, with weapons of righteousness, through glory and dishonor, through slander and praise; regarded as impostors, and yet true; as unknown, and yet well-known; as dying and yet we continue to live; as those who are scourged and yet not executed; as sorrowful, but always rejoicing, as poor, but making many rich, as having nothing, and yet possessing everything.

We have spoken freely to you, Corinthians; our heart has been opened wide to you. Open your hearts to us also.

Do not become partners with those who do not believe, for what fellowship does light have with darkness or what does a believer share in common with an unbeliever? What mutual agreement does the temple of God have with idols? We are the temple of the living God, therefore "**come out from their midst, and be separate**," says the Lord.

Therefore, since we have these promises, dear friends, let us cleanse ourselves from everything that could defile the body and the spirit, out of reverence for God. Make room for us in your hearts; we have wronged no one, we have *exploited no one. I do not say this to condemn you, for I told you before that you are in our hearts so that we die together and live together with you.*

I have great confidence in you. I am overflowing with joy in the midst of all our suffering. When we came into Macedonia we were troubled in every way – struggles from the outside, fears from within. But God encouraged us by the arrival of Titus. We were encouraged not only by his arrival, but also by the encouragement you gave him, as he reported to us your longing, your mourning, your deep concern for me, so that I rejoiced more than ever.

Even if I made you sad by my letter,[28] I do not regret having written it (even though I did regret it, for I see that my letter made you sad, though only for a short time). Now I rejoice, not because you were made sad, but because you were made sad to the point of repentance. Sadness as intended by God produces a repentance that leads to salvation. You have proved yourselves to be innocent in this matter, therefore we have been encouraged. We rejoiced even more at the joy of Titus, because all of you have refreshed his spirit. Just as everything we said to you was true, so our boasting to Titus about you has proved true as well. His affection for you is much greater when he remembers how you welcomed him.

Now we make known to you the grace of God given to the churches of Macedonia, that during a severe ordeal of suffering, their abundant joy and their extreme poverty have overflowed in their generosity. They gave beyond their means. They did so voluntarily, begging us for the blessing of helping the saints. They did this not just as we had hoped, but they gave themselves first to the Lord and to us by the will of God.

Thus we urged Titus that just as he had previously begun this work, so also he should complete this act of

28   Paul is talking about his "harsh letter" to the Corinthians. This letter has never been found.

kindness for you. As you excel in everything – in faith, in speech, in knowledge – make sure that you excel in this act of kindness too. You know the grace of our Lord Jesus Christ, that although he was rich, he became poor for your sakes, so that you by his poverty could become rich.

It is to your advantage, since you made a good start last year both in your giving and your desire to give, to finish what you started. If the eagerness is present, the gift itself is acceptable according to whatever one has, not according to what he does not have. I do not say this so there would be relief for others and suffering for you, but as a matter of equality. At the present time, your abundance will meet their need so that one day their abundance may also meet your need.

Thanks be to God who put in the heart of Titus the same devotion I have for you because he not only accepted our request but he is coming to you of his own accord. We are sending along with him the brother who is praised by all the churches for his work in spreading the gospel. This brother has also been chosen by the churches as our traveling companion as we administer this generous gift to the glory of the Lord and to show our readiness to help.

We did this as a precaution so that no one should blame us in regard to this generous gift we are administering. We are concerned about what is right not only before the Lord but also before men and we are sending with them our brother whom we have tested many times. I thought it necessary to urge these brothers to go to you in advance and to arrange ahead of time the generous contribution you had promised, so this may be ready as a generous gift and not as something you feel forced to do.

My point is this: The person who sows sparingly will also reap sparingly, and the person who sows generously will also reap generously. Each one of you should give just as he has decided in his heart, not reluctantly or under compulsion, because God loves a cheerful giver.

The service of this ministry is not only providing for the needs of the saints but is also overflowing with many thanks to God. Thanks be to God for his indescribable gift!

Chapter Five

Paul's Third Journey: Romans

Introduction to Romans

After sending Titus to deliver Second Corinthians, Paul continued his ministry in Macedonia. In Paul's letter to the Romans (below) Paul says that he had ministered all the way to Illyricum (northwest of Macedonia) and it is likely that his Illyricum ministry occurred at this time as well. Then Paul traveled back to Corinth where he stayed for three months.

In AD 57, while in Corinth, Paul wrote his letter to the church at Rome, a church he had never visited. He wrote to explain his Gospel to the Christians in Rome and to ask for their prayer and financial support for a ministry he was planning to Spain.

Paul's letter to the Romans is his most "theological" letter. He systematically spells out his Gospel of salvation by grace through faith in Jesus Christ. Paul explains how his gospel relates to Jewish Law, i.e. what Christians call, The Old Testament, especially the "the Law of Moses", Genesis, Exodus, Leviticus, Numbers and Deuteronomy. This is important because Paul sees his gospel as the fulfillment of that which Moses and the Jewish prophets predicted. The essence of Paul's letter to the Romans appears below.

From Paul, a slave of Christ Jesus, called to be an apostle, set apart for the gospel of God. This gospel he promised in the Holy Scriptures, concerning his Son who was a descendant of David, appointed the Son-of-God-in-power by the resurrection from the dead, Jesus Christ our Lord. Through him we have received grace and our apostleship to bring about the obedience of faith among the Gentiles. To those loved by God in Rome, called saints: Grace and peace to you from God our Father and the Lord Jesus Christ!

I thank God for all of you because your faith is proclaimed throughout the whole world. God is my witness that I ask in my prayers, if perhaps I may succeed in visiting you so that we may be mutually comforted by one another's faith.

I do not want you to be unaware, brothers and sisters that I often intended to come to you (and was prevented until now), so that I may have some fruit even among you, just as I already have among the rest of the Gentiles. I am eager also to preach the gospel to you who are in Rome.

*I am not ashamed of the gospel, for it is God's power for salvation to everyone who believes, to the Jew first and also to the Greek. For the righteousness of God is revealed in the gospel from faith to faith, as it is written, "**The righteous by faith will live.**"*

The wrath of God is revealed against all ungodliness and unrighteousness of people who suppress the truth by their unrighteousness. What can be known about God is plain to them because God has made it plain to them. Since the creation of the world his eternal power and divine nature have been understood through what has been made so people are without excuse. Although they knew God they did not glorify him or give him thanks, but they became futile in their thoughts and their senseless hearts were darkened. Although they claimed to be wise, they became fools and exchanged the glory of the immortal God for an image resembling human beings, birds, animals or reptiles.

Therefore God gave them over in the desires of their hearts to impurity, to dishonor their bodies among themselves. They exchanged the truth of God for a lie and worshiped and served the creation rather than the Creator, who is blessed forever!

For this reason God gave them over to dishonorable passions. Their women exchanged natural sexual relations for unnatural ones, and likewise the men also abandoned natural relations with women and were inflamed in their passions for one another. Men committed shameless acts with men and received in themselves the due penalty for their error.

As they did not see fit to acknowledge God, God gave them over to a depraved mind, to do what should not be done. They are filled with every kind of unrighteousness, wickedness, covetousness, malice, envy, murder, strife, deceit, hostility. They are gossips, slanderers, haters of God, insolent, arrogant, boastful, contrivers of all sorts of evil, disobedient to parents, senseless, covenant-breakers, heartless, ruthless. Although they fully know God's righteous decree that those who practice such things deserve to die, they not only do them but also approve of those who practice them.

Therefore you are without excuse when you judge someone else. For on whatever grounds you judge another, you condemn yourself, because you practice the same things. Do you think when you judge those who practice such things and yet do them yourself, that you will escape God's judgment?

Do you not know that God's kindness leads you to repentance? Because of your unrepentant heart, you are storing up wrath for yourselves in the day of wrath, when God's righteous judgment is revealed! He **will reward each one according to his works**: eternal life to those who by perseverance in good works seek glory and honor and immortality, but wrath and anger to those who live in selfish ambition and unrighteousness. There will be affliction and distress on everyone who does evil, but glory and honor and peace for everyone who does good, for the Jew first and also the Greek

.There is no partiality with God. All who have sinned apart from the law will perish apart from the law, and all who have sinned under the law will be judged by the law. It is not those who hear the law who are righteous before God, but those who do the law will be declared righteous.

Whenever the Gentiles who do not have the law, do by nature the things required by the law, they show that the work of the law is written in their hearts. Their conscience bears witness and their conflicting thoughts accuse or defend them on the day when God will judge the secrets of human hearts, according to my gospel through Christ Jesus.

But if you call yourself a Jew and rely on the law and boast of your relationship to God and if you are convinced that you are a light to those who are in darkness, an educator of the senseless, – therefore you who teach someone else, do you not teach yourself? You who preach against stealing, do you steal? You who tell others not to commit adultery, do you commit adultery? You who boast in the law dishonor God by transgressing the law!

If you break the law your circumcision has become uncircumcision.[29] Therefore if the uncircumcised man obeys the righteous requirements of the law, will not his uncircumcision be regarded as circumcision? A person is not a Jew who is one outwardly but someone is a Jew who is one inwardly, and circumcision is of the heart by the Spirit.

Therefore what advantage does the Jew have or

---

29   Circumcision was a sign of the Covenant relationship God has established with the Jewish people, but even Jewish people could be cut off from that relationship if they broke God's Covenant.

what is the value of circumcision? Actually, there are many advantages. First of all, the Jews were entrusted with the oracles of God. What then? If some did not believe, does their unbelief nullify the faithfulness of God? Absolutely not! If our unrighteousness demonstrates the righteousness of God, why not say, "Let us do evil so that good may come of it"? – as some who slander us allege that we say (Their condemnation is deserved)!

What then? Are we better off? Certainly not, for we have already charged that Jews and Greeks alike are all under sin, just as it is written:

"There is no one righteous, not even one. There is no one who seeks God. All have turned away. "Their throats are open graves, they deceive with their tongues, the poison of asps is under their lips." "Their mouths are full of cursing and bitterness." "Their feet are swift to shed blood, ruin and misery are in their paths, and the way of peace they have not known." "There is no fear of God before their eyes."

Now we know that whatever the law says, it says so that every mouth may be silenced and the whole world may be held accountable to God. No one is declared righteous by the works of the law for through the law comes the knowledge of sin.

But now apart from the law the righteousness of God (which is attested by the law and the prophets) has been disclosed – namely, the righteousness of God through the faithfulness of Jesus Christ for all who believe. There is no distinction, for all have sinned and fall short of the glory of God. They are justified freely by his grace through the redemption that is in Christ Jesus. This was to demonstrate his righteousness, because God in his forbearance had passed over the sins previously committed. This was also to demonstrate his righteousness in the present time, so that he would be just and the justifier of the one who lives because of Jesus' faithfulness.

Where, then, is boasting?

It is excluded!

By what principle? Of works?

No, but by the principle of faith!

Do we then nullify the law through faith?

Absolutely not! Instead we uphold the law. For what does the scripture say? **"Abraham believed God, and it was credited to him as righteousness."** Now to the one who works, his pay is not credited due to grace but due to obligation. But to the one who does not work, but believes in the one who declares the ungodly righteous, his faith is credited as righteousness.

Even David speaks regarding the blessedness of the man to whom God credits righteousness apart from works: **"Blessed are those whose lawless deeds are forgiven, and whose sins are covered; blessed is the one against whom the Lord will never count sin."**

Is this blessedness then for the circumcision or also for the uncircumcision? We say, **"faith was credited to** Abraham **as righteousness."** Was he circumcised at the time?

No, he was not circumcised! He received the sign of circumcision as a seal of the righteousness that he had by faith, so that he would become the father of all those who believe but have never been circumcised, that they too could have righteousness credited to them. He is also the father of the circumcised who are not only circumcised, but who also walk in the footsteps of the faith that our father Abraham possessed.

The promise to Abraham or to his descendants that he would inherit the world was fulfilled through the righteousness that comes by faith. The law brings wrath because where there is no law there is no transgression. For this reason it [the promise] is by faith so that it may be by grace, with the result that the promise may be certain to all the descendants

– not only to those who are under the law, but also to those who have the faith of Abraham.

*Abraham believed with the result that he became **the father of many nations**. He was fully convinced that what God promised he was also able to do. So indeed it was credited to Abraham as righteousness.*

Therefore, since we have been declared righteous by faith, we have peace with God through our Lord Jesus Christ and we rejoice in the hope of God's glory. Not only this, but we also rejoice in sufferings, knowing that suffering produces endurance, and endurance, character, and character, hope. Hope does not disappoint because the love of God has been poured out in our hearts through the Holy Spirit who was given to us.

While we were still helpless Christ died for the ungodly. God demonstrates his own love for us in that while we were still sinners, Christ died for us. Because we have now been declared righteous by his blood, we will be saved through him from God's wrath. For if while we were enemies we were reconciled to God through the death of his Son, how much more, since we have been reconciled, will we be saved by his life? We also rejoice in God through our Lord Jesus Christ through whom we have now received this reconciliation.

So then, just as sin entered the world through one man and death through sin, and so death spread to all people because all sinned. But the gracious gift is not like the transgression. For if the many died through the transgression of the one man, how much more did the grace of God and the gift by the grace of the one man Jesus Christ multiply to the many!

The gift is not like the one who sinned. For judgment, resulting from the one transgression led to condemnation, but the gracious gift led to justification. For if, by the transgression of the one man, death reigned, how much more will those who receive grace and of the gift of righteousness reign in life through the one, Jesus Christ!

Just as condemnation for all people came through one transgression, so too through the one righteous act came righteousness leading to life for all people.

Just as through the disobedience of the one man many were made sinners, so also through the obedience of one man many will be made righteous. The law came in so that the transgression may increase, but where sin increased grace multiplied all the more

Just as sin reigned in death, so also grace will reign through righteousness to eternal life through Jesus Christ our Lord.

What shall we say then? Are we to remain in sin so that grace may increase? Absolutely not! How can we who died to sin still live in it? Do you not know that as many as were baptized into Christ Jesus were baptized into his death? Therefore we have been buried with him through baptism into death in order that just as Christ was raised from the dead, so we too may live a new life.

For if we have become united with him in the likeness of his death, we will certainly also be united in the likeness of his resurrection. We know that our old man was crucified with him so that we would no longer be enslaved to sin.

Now if we died with Christ, we believe that we will also live with him. We know that since Christ has been raised from the dead, he is never going to die again. He died to sin once for all, but the life he lives, he lives to God. So you too consider yourselves dead to sin but alive to God in Christ Jesus.

Therefore do not let sin reign in your body. Do not present your members to sin as instruments to be used for unrighteousness, but present yourselves to God and your members to God as instruments to be used for righteousness. Sin will have no mastery over you because you are not under law but under grace.

What then? Shall we sin because we are not under law but under grace? Absolutely not! Do you not know that you are slaves of the one you obey, either of sin resulting in death, or obedience resulting in righteousness? Thanks be to God that though you were slaves to sin, you obeyed from the heart and having been freed from sin, you became enslaved to righteousness. Just as you once presented your members as slaves to impurity and lawlessness leading to more lawlessness, so now present your members as slaves to righteousness leading to sanctification.

The payoff of sin is death but the gift of God is eternal life in Christ Jesus our Lord. The law is lord over a person as long as he lives. For a married woman is bound by law to her husband as long as he lives, but if her husband dies, she is released from the law of the marriage. You also died to the law through the body of Christ, so that you could be joined to the one who was raised from the dead, to bear fruit to God.

When we were in the flesh, the sinful desires, aroused by the law were active in the members of our body to bear fruit for death. But now we have been released from the law so that we may serve in the new life of the Spirit and not under the old written code.

*What shall we say then? Is the law sin? Absolutely not! I would not have known sin except through the law. I would not have known what it means to desire something belonging to someone else if the law had not said, "**Do not covet**." But sin, through the commandment, produced in me all kinds of wrong desires. I was once alive apart from the law but with the coming of the commandment sin became alive and I died. I found that the very commandment that was intended to bring life brought death! For sin, seizing the opportunity through the commandment deceived me and I died. So then, the law is holy, and the commandment is holy, righteous, and good.*

Did that which is good, then, become death to me?

Absolutely not! But sin, so that it would be shown to be sin, produced death in me through what is good, so that through the commandment sin would become utterly sinful. We know that the law is spiritual – but I am unspiritual, sold into slavery to sin.

I don't understand what I am doing. I do not do what I want – instead, I do what I hate. If I do what I don't want, I agree that the law is good. I want to do good but I cannot do it. I do not do the good I want but I do the very evil I do not want! I find that when I want to do good, evil is present with me.

I delight in the law of God in my inner being, but I see a different law making me captive to the law of sin that is in my members. Wretched man that I am! Who will rescue me from this body of death? Thanks be to God through Jesus Christ our Lord! So then, I myself serve the law of God with my mind, but with my flesh I serve the law of sin.

There is therefore now no condemnation for those who are in Christ Jesus. For the law of the life-giving Spirit in Christ Jesus has set you free from the law of sin and death. God achieved what the law could not do because it was weakened through the flesh. By sending his own Son in the likeness of sinful flesh, he condemned sin in the flesh, so that the righteous requirement of the law may be fulfilled in us who walk according to the Spirit.

Those who live according to the flesh have their outlook shaped by the things of the flesh, but those who live according to the Spirit have their outlook shaped by the things of the Spirit.

The outlook of the flesh is death but the outlook of the Spirit is life and peace.

The outlook of the flesh is hostile to God, for it does not submit to the law of God nor is it able to do so. Those who are in the flesh cannot please God.

You, however, are not in the flesh but in the Spirit, if indeed the Spirit of God lives in you. If anyone does not have the Spirit of Christ, this person does not belong to him. Moreover if the Spirit of the one who raised Jesus from the dead lives in you, the one who raised Christ from the dead will also make your mortal bodies alive through his Spirit who lives in you.

So then, brothers and sisters, if you live according to the flesh, you will die, but if by the Spirit you put to death the deeds of the body you will live. For all who are led by the Spirit of God are the sons of God. You did not receive the spirit of slavery leading again to fear, but you received the Spirit of adoption, by whom we cry, "Abba, Father." The Spirit himself bears witness to our spirit that we are God's children, heirs of God and also fellow heirs with Christ – if indeed we suffer with him so we may also be glorified with him.

I consider that our present sufferings cannot even be compared to the glory that will be revealed to us. The creation eagerly waits for the revelation of the sons of God. The creation was subjected to futility – not willingly but because of God who subjected it – in hope that the creation itself will also be set free from the bondage of decay into the glorious freedom of God's children. We know that the whole creation groans and suffers together until now. We ourselves also groan inwardly as we eagerly await the redemption of our bodies.

The Spirit helps us in our weakness, for we do not know how we should pray, but the Spirit himself intercedes for us with inexpressible groanings. We know that all things work together for good for those who love God, who are called according to his purpose, because those whom he foreknew he also predestined to be conformed to the image of his Son. Those he predestined, he also called; and those he called, he also justified; and those he justified, he also glorified.

If God is for us, who can be against us? Indeed, he who

did not spare his own Son – how will he not also freely give us all things? Who will bring any charge against God's elect? It is God who justifies. Who is the one who will condemn? Christ is the one who was raised and who is interceding for us. Who will separate us from the love of Christ? Will trouble, or distress, or persecution, or famine, or nakedness, or danger, or sword? No, in all these things we have complete victory through him who loved us! I am convinced that neither death, nor life, nor things that are present, nor things to come, nor powers, nor anything else in creation will be able to separate us from the love of God in Christ Jesus our Lord.

I am telling the truth in Christ – I have unceasing anguish in my heart, for I could wish that I myself were accursed for the sake of my people who are Israelites. To them belong the glory, the covenants, the giving of the law, the temple worship, the promises, the patriarchs, and from them came the Christ, who is God over all, blessed forever!

It is not as though the word of God had failed, for not all those who are descended from Israel are truly Israel nor are all Abraham's true descendants. It is not the children of the flesh who are the children of God; rather, the children of promise are counted as descendants.

This is what the promise declared: **"About a year from now I will return and Sarah will have a son."** *When Rebekah had conceived children by our ancestor Isaac – even before they were born or had done anything good or bad (so that God's purpose in election would stand, not by works but by his calling) it was said to her,* **"The older will serve the younger,"** *just as it is written:* **"Jacob I loved, but Esau I hated."**

What shall we say then? Is there injustice with God? Absolutely not! He says to Moses: **"I will have mercy on whom I have mercy, and I will have compassion on whom I have compassion."** *So then, it does not depend on human desire or exertion but on God who shows mercy. The scripture says to Pharaoh:* **"For this very purpose I have raised you up, that**

I may demonstrate my power in you, and that my name may be proclaimed in all the earth." God has mercy on whom he chooses to have mercy and he hardens whom he chooses to harden.

You will say to me then, "Why does he still find fault for who has ever resisted his will?" But who are you to talk back to God? Has the potter no right to make from the same lump of clay one vessel for special use and another for ordinary use?

What if God has endured with much patience the objects of wrath prepared for destruction? What if he is willing to make known the wealth of his glory on the objects of mercy that he has prepared beforehand for glory – even us, whom he has called, not only from the Jews but also from the Gentiles?

What shall we say then? – that the Gentiles who did not pursue righteousness obtained it, that is, a righteousness that is by faith, but Israel even though pursuing a law of righteousness did not attain it. Why not? Because they pursued it not by faith but by works.

Brothers and sisters, my heart's desire and prayer to God on behalf of my fellow Israelites is for their salvation. I can testify that they are zealous for God but their zeal is not in line with the truth. Seeking to establish their own righteousness, they did not submit to God's righteousness.

Christ is the end of the law, with the result that there is righteousness for everyone who believes. If you confess with your mouth that Jesus is Lord and believe in your heart that God raised him from the dead, you will be saved. With the heart one believes and thus has righteousness and with the mouth one confesses and thus has salvation. There is no distinction between the Jew and the Greek for the same Lord is Lord of all, who richly blesses all who call on him. For **everyone who calls on the name of the Lord will be saved.**

*How are they to call on one they have not believed in? And how are they to believe in one they have not heard of? How are they to hear without someone preaching to them? How are they to preach unless they are sent? Not all have obeyed the good news, for Isaiah says, "**Lord, who has believed our report**?" Faith comes from what is heard and what is heard comes through the preached word of Christ.*

*Have they not heard? Yes, they have. Didn't Israel understand? First Moses says, "**I will make you jealous by those who are not a nation.**" Isaiah is even bold enough to say, "**I was found by those who did not seek me.**" But about Israel he says, "**All day long I held out my hands to this disobedient and stubborn people!**"*

*So I ask, God has not rejected his people, has he? Absolutely not! I too am an Israelite, a descendant of Abraham, from the tribe of Benjamin. God has not rejected his people whom he foreknew! Do you not know what the scripture says about Elijah, how he pleads with God against Israel? "Lord, **they have killed your prophets, they have demolished your altars; I alone am left and they are seeking my life!**" But what was the divine response to him? "**I have kept for myself seven thousand people who have not bent the knee to Baal.**"*

In the same way at the present time there is a remnant chosen by grace. And if it is by grace, it is no longer by works, otherwise grace would no longer be grace.

*What then? Israel failed to obtain what it was diligently seeking but the elect obtained it. The rest were hardened, as it is written, "**God gave them a spirit of stupor, eyes that would not see and ears that would not hear, to this very day.**"*

They did not stumble into an irrevocable fall, did they? Absolutely not! But by their transgression salvation has come to the Gentiles, to make Israel jealous. Now if their transgression means riches for the world and their defeat means riches for the Gentiles, how much more will their full restoration bring?

Seeing that I am an apostle to the Gentiles, I magnify my ministry, if somehow I could provoke my people to jealousy and save some of them. If their rejection is the reconciliation of the world, what will their acceptance be but life from the dead?

If the root is holy, so too are the branches. If some of the branches were broken off, and you, a wild olive shoot, were grafted in among them and participated in the richness of the olive root, do not boast over the branches. Remember that the root supports you!

Then you will say, "The branches were broken off so that I could be grafted in." Granted! They were broken off because of their unbelief but you stand by faith. Do not be arrogant, but fear! If God did not spare the natural branches, perhaps he will not spare you.

Notice therefore the kindness and harshness of God – harshness toward those who have fallen, but God's kindness toward you, provided you continue in his kindness; otherwise you also will be cut off. And they – if they do not continue in their unbelief – will be grafted in.

I do not want you to be ignorant of this mystery, brothers and sisters: A partial hardening has happened to Israel until the full number of the Gentiles has come in, and so all Israel will be saved.

In regard to the gospel they are enemies for your sake, but in regard to election they are dearly loved for the sake of the fathers, for the gifts and the call of God are irrevocable. Just as you were formerly disobedient to God, but have now received mercy so they too may now receive mercy. God has consigned all people to disobedience so that he may show mercy to all.

Oh, the depth of the riches and wisdom and knowledge

of God! How unsearchable are his judgments and how fathomless his ways! For from him and through him and to him are all things. To him be glory forever!

Therefore I exhort you, brothers and sisters, by the mercies of God, to present your bodies as a sacrifice – alive, holy, and pleasing to God – which is your reasonable service. Do not be conformed to this world but be transformed by the renewing of your mind so that you may test and approve what is the will of God – what is good and well-pleasing and perfect.

I say to every one of you not to think more highly of yourself than you ought to think but to think with sober discernment. Just as in one body we have many members, so we who are many are one body in Christ. We have different gifts according to the grace given to us. If the gift is prophecy, that individual must use it in proportion to his faith. If it is service, he must serve; if it is teaching, he must teach; if it is exhortation, he must exhort; if it is contributing, he must do so with sincerity; if it is leadership, he must do so with diligence; if it is showing mercy, he must do so with cheerfulness.

Love must be without hypocrisy. Abhor what is evil, cling to what is good. Be devoted to one another with mutual love. Do not lag in zeal, be enthusiastic in spirit, serve the Lord. Rejoice in hope, endure in suffering, persist in prayer. Contribute to the needs of the saints, pursue hospitality. Bless those who persecute you and do not curse. Rejoice with those who rejoice, weep with those who weep. Live in harmony with one another; do not be haughty but associate with the lowly. Do not be conceited.

*Do not repay anyone evil for evil; consider what is good before all people. If possible, so far as it depends on you, live peaceably with all people. Do not avenge yourselves but give place to God's wrath, for it is written, "**Vengeance is mine, I will repay,**" says the Lord. Rather, **if your enemy is hungry, feed him; if he is thirsty, give him a drink; for in doing this***

you will be heaping burning coals on his head*. Do not be
overcome by evil, but overcome evil with good.*

*Let every person be subject to the governing
authorities for the authorities that exist have been instituted
by God. The person who resists such authority resists the
ordinance of God and those who resist will incur judgment
for it is God's servant for your good. But if you do wrong, be in
fear, for it does not bear the sword in vain. It is God's servant
to administer retribution on the wrongdoer. Therefore be in
subjection, not only because of the wrath of the authorities
but also because of your conscience. Pay everyone what
is owed: taxes to whom taxes are due, revenue to whom
revenue is due, respect to whom respect is due, honor to
whom honor is due.*

*Owe no one anything, except to love one another,
for the one who loves his neighbor has fulfilled the law. The
commandments are summed up in this, "****Love your neighbor
as yourself.****" Love does no wrong to a neighbor. Therefore
love is the fulfillment of the law.*

*Lay aside the works of darkness and put on the
weapons of light. Live decently as in the daytime, not in
carousing and drunkenness, not in sexual immorality and
sensuality, not in discord and jealousy. Instead, put on the
Lord Jesus Christ and make no provision for the flesh to
arouse its desires.*

*Receive the one who is weak in the faith. One person
believes in eating everything but the weak person eats only
vegetables. The one who eats everything must not despise
the one who does not, and the one who abstains must not
judge the one who eats everything, for God has accepted
him. Who are you to pass judgment on another's servant?
Before his own master he stands or falls, and he will stand,
for the Lord is able to make him stand.*

*One person regards one day holier than other days and
another regards them all alike. Each must be fully convinced*

in his own mind. The one who observes the day does it for the Lord. The one who eats, eats for the Lord, and the one who abstains from eating abstains for the Lord. If we live, we live for the Lord; if we die, we die for the Lord. Therefore, whether we live or die, we are the Lord's. For this reason Christ died and returned to life, so that he may be the Lord of both the dead and the living.

*But you who eat vegetables only – why do you judge your brother or sister? And you who eat everything – why do you despise your brother or sister? For we will all stand before the judgment seat of God. For it is written, "**As I live, says the Lord, every knee will bow to me, and every tongue will give praise to God**." Therefore, each of us will give an account of himself to God.*

Therefore determine never to place an obstacle or a trap before a brother or sister. I know that there is nothing unclean in itself; still, it is unclean to the one who considers it unclean. If your brother or sister is distressed because of what you eat, you are no longer walking in love. Do not destroy by your food someone for whom Christ died. The one who serves Christ in this way is pleasing to God and approved by people.

So then, let us pursue what makes for peace and for building up one another. Do not destroy the work of God for the sake of food. Although all things are clean, it is wrong to cause anyone to stumble by what you eat. It is good not to eat meat or drink wine or to do anything that causes your brother to stumble. The man who doubts is condemned if he eats, because he does not do so from faith, and whatever is not from faith is sin.

*We who are strong ought to bear with the failings of the weak, and not just please ourselves. Let each of us please his neighbor for his good to build him up. For even Christ did not please himself, but just as it is written, "**The insults of those who insult you have fallen on me**." Everything that* *was written in former times was written for our instruction so that through encouragement of the scriptures we may have hope. Now may the God of endurance and comfort give you unity with one another in accordance with Christ Jesus, so that together you may with one voice glorify the God and Father of our Lord Jesus Christ. Receive one another, then, just as Christ also received you.*

I serve the gospel of God like a priest, so that the Gentiles may become an acceptable offering, sanctified by the Holy Spirit. I boast in Christ Jesus about the things that pertain to God. I will not dare to speak of anything except what Christ has accomplished through me in order to bring about the obedience of the Gentiles, by word and deed, in the power of signs and wonders, in the power of the Spirit of God. So from Jerusalem even as far as Illyricum I have fully preached the gospel of Christ. I desire to preach where Christ has not been named so as not to build on another person's foundation.

This is the reason I was often hindered from coming to you. There is nothing more to keep me in these regions and I have for many years desired to come to you when I go to Spain. I hope to visit you and that you will help me on my journey there, after I have enjoyed your company for a while.

Now I go to Jerusalem to minister to the saints, for Macedonia and Achaia are pleased to make some contribution for the poor among the saints in Jerusalem. If the Gentiles have shared in their spiritual things, they are obligated also to minister to them in material things. Therefore after I have completed this and have safely delivered this bounty to them, I will set out for Spain by way of you.

Pray that I may be rescued from those who are disobedient in Judea and that my ministry in Jerusalem may be acceptable to the saints, so that by God's will I may come to you with joy and be refreshed in your company. Now may the God of peace be with all of you.

I commend to you our sister Phoebe who is a servant of the church in Cenchrea. Welcome her in the Lord in a way worthy of the saints and provide her with whatever help she may need from you, for she has been a great help to many, including me.

Greet Prisca and Aquila, my fellow workers in Christ Jesus, who risked their own necks for my life. Also greet the church in their house. Greet Mary, who has worked very hard for you. Greet Andronicus and Junia, my compatriots and my fellow prisoners. They are well known to the apostles, and they were in Christ before me. Greet Rufus, chosen in the Lord, and his mother who was also a mother to me. Greet Philologus and Julia, Nereus and his sister, and Olympas, and all the believers who are with them. Greet one another with a holy kiss. All the churches of Christ greet you.

Watch out for those who create dissensions and obstacles contrary to the teaching that you learned. Avoid them! I want you to be wise in what is good and innocent in what is evil. The God of peace will quickly crush Satan under your feet. The grace of our Lord Jesus be with you.

Timothy, my fellow worker, greets you; so do Lucius, Jason, and Sosipater, my compatriots. I, Tertius, who am writing this letter, greet you in the Lord. Gaius, who is host to me and to the whole church, greets you.

Now to him who is able to strengthen you according to my gospel and the proclamation of Jesus Christ, and through the prophetic scriptures has been made known to all the nations, according to the command of the eternal God, to bring about the obedience of faith – to the only wise God, through Jesus Christ, be glory forever! Amen.

CHAPTER SIX

From Corinth, to Jerusalem, to Rome[30]

From Corinth to Jerusalem

Paul was preparing to sail from Corinth when he discovered a plot by some Jews against his life, so he decided to return through Macedonia. Several men were traveling with him: Sopater of Berea, Aristarchus and Secundus, from Thessalonica; Gaius, from Derbe; Timothy; and Tychicus and Trophimus, who were from the province of Asia. They went ahead and waited for us at Troas. As soon as the Passover season ended, we boarded a ship at Philippi in Macedonia and five days later arrived in Troas where we stayed a week.

On the first day of the week we gathered to observe the Lord's Supper. Paul was preaching and, since he was leaving the next day, he talked until midnight. As Paul spoke on and on a young man named Eutychus, sitting on the windowsill, sank into a deep sleep and fell three stories to his death below.

Paul went down and took him into his arms. "Don't worry," he said, "he's alive!" Then they all went back upstairs and ate the Lord's Supper together. Paul continued talking to them until dawn; then he left. Meanwhile, the young man was taken home unhurt and everyone was greatly relieved.

Paul went by land to Assos and we went on ahead by ship. He joined us there and we sailed together to Mitylene.

30   From Acts 20-21.

The next day we passed the island of Kios. The following day, we crossed to the island of Samos and a day later we arrived at Miletus. Paul had decided against stopping at Ephesus this time. He was hurrying to get to Jerusalem for the Festival of Pentecost.

When we landed at Miletus, he sent a message to the elders of the church at Ephesus, asking them to come down to meet him. When they arrived he declared,

"I have had one message for Jews and Gentiles alike, the necessity of turning from sin and turning to God, and of faith in our Lord Jesus. Now I am going to Jerusalem, drawn there irresistibly by the Holy Spirit, not knowing what awaits me except that the Holy Spirit has told me in city after city that jail and suffering lie ahead. My life is worth nothing unless I use it for the work of telling others the Good News about God's wonderful kindness and love. None of you will ever see me again. Be sure that you shepherd God's flock, his church, purchased with his blood, over whom the Holy Spirit has appointed you as elders. False teachers, like vicious wolves, will come in among you after I leave. Remember the three years I was with you, my constant care over you and my many tears for you. Now I entrust you to God and the word of his grace. I have never coveted anyone's money or fine clothing. You know that these hands of mine have worked to pay my own way and I have even supplied the needs of those who were with me. I have been a constant example of how you can help the poor by working hard. You should remember the words of the Lord Jesus: 'It is more blessed to give than to receive.'"

When he had finished speaking, he knelt and prayed with them. They wept aloud as they embraced him in farewell, sad most of all because he had said that they would never see him again. Then they accompanied him down to the ship.

We sailed to the island of Cos, the next day we reached Rhodes and then went to Patara. There we boarded a ship sailing for the Syrian province of Phoenicia. We landed at the harbor of Tyre in Syria, where the ship was to unload.

We went ashore, found the local believers and stayed with them a week. These disciples prophesied through the Holy Spirit that Paul should not go on to Jerusalem. When we returned to the ship at the end of the week the entire congregation including wives and children came down to the shore with us. There we knelt, prayed, and said our farewells. The next stop after leaving Tyre was Ptolemais where we greeted the brothers and sisters but stayed only one day.

Then we went on to Caesarea and stayed at the home of Philip the Evangelist, one of the seven men who had been chosen to distribute food. He had four unmarried daughters who had the gift of prophecy. During our stay of several days a man named Agabus, who also had the gift of prophecy, arrived from Judea. When he visited us, he took Paul's belt and bound his own feet and hands with it. Then he said, "The Holy Spirit declares, 'So shall the owner of this belt be bound by the Jewish leaders in Jerusalem and turned over to the Romans."

We begged Paul not to go on to Jerusalem, but he said, "Why all this weeping? You are breaking my heart! I am ready not only to be jailed at Jerusalem but also to die for the sake of the Lord Jesus." When it was clear that we couldn't persuade him we gave up and said, "The will of the Lord be done."

Paul's Arrest in Jerusalem[31]

Shortly afterward we left for Jerusalem. Some believers from Caesarea accompanied us and took us to the home of Mnason, one of the early disciples. The brothers and sisters in Jerusalem welcomed us cordially. The next day Paul went in with us to meet with James, and all the elders of the Jerusalem church were present. Paul gave a detailed account of the things God had accomplished among the Gentiles

31   From Acts 21-24.

through his ministry. After hearing this, they praised God but said,

You know, brother, how many thousands of Jews have also believed and they all take the Law of Moses very seriously. Our Jewish Christians here at Jerusalem have been told that you are teaching the Jews to turn their backs on the laws of Moses. They say that you teach people not to circumcise their children or follow other Jewish customs. Here's our suggestion. We have four men here who have taken a vow and are preparing to shave their heads. Go with them to the Temple, join them in the purification ceremony, and pay for them to have their heads shaved. Then everyone will know that the rumors are all false and that you yourself observe the Jewish laws. As for the Gentile Christians, all we ask of them is what we already told them in a letter: They should not eat food offered to idols, nor consume blood, nor eat meat from strangled animals, and they should stay away from all sexual immorality.

Paul agreed to their request. The next day he went through the purification ritual with the men and went to the Temple. Then he publicly announced the date when their vows would end and sacrifices would be offered for each of them.

The seven days were almost ended when some Jews from the province of Asia saw Paul in the Temple and roused a mob against him. They grabbed him, yelling, "This is the man who tells everybody to disobey the Jewish laws. He speaks against the Temple and he even defiles it by bringing Gentiles in!" (Earlier that day they had seen him in the city with Trophimus, a Gentile from Ephesus, and they assumed Paul had taken him into the Temple).

A riot followed. Paul was dragged out of the Temple. As they were trying to kill him, word reached the commander of the Roman regiment that Jerusalem was in an uproar. He immediately called out his soldiers and ran down among the crowd. The commander arrested him and asked the crowd what he had done. He couldn't find out the truth in all the confusion, so he ordered Paul to be taken to the fortress. The crowd followed behind shouting, "Kill him, kill him!"

As Paul was about to be taken inside he said to the commander, "May I have a word with you?" "Do you know Greek?" the commander asked, surprised. "Aren't you the Egyptian who led a rebellion some time ago and took four thousand members of the Assassins out into the desert?"

"No," Paul replied, "I am a Jew from Tarsus in Cilicia. Please, let me talk to these people."

The commander agreed so Paul stood on the stairs and motioned to the people to be quiet. Soon a deep silence enveloped the crowd and he addressed them in their own language, Aramaic.

"Brothers and esteemed fathers," Paul said, "listen to me as I offer my defense." When they heard him speaking in their own language, the silence was even greater.

I am a Jew, born in Tarsus. I was brought up and educated here in Jerusalem under Gamaliel. I became very zealous to honor God in everything I did and I persecuted the followers of the Way, hounding some to death, binding and delivering both men and women to prison. The high priest and the whole council of leaders can testify that this is so for I received letters from them authorizing me to bring the Christians from there to Jerusalem, in chains to be punished. As I was nearing Damascus, about noon a very bright light from heaven suddenly shone around me. I fell to the ground and heard a voice saying to me, "Saul, Saul, why are you persecuting me?" "Who are you, sir?" I asked. He replied, "I am Jesus of Nazareth, the one you are persecuting." After I returned to Jerusalem I was praying in the Temple and I saw a vision of Jesus saying to me, "Hurry! Leave Jerusalem, for the people here won't believe you when you give them your testimony about me." "But Lord," I argued, "they certainly know that I imprisoned and beat those in every synagogue who believed on you. When your witness Stephen was killed, I was standing there agreeing." But the Lord said to me, "Leave Jerusalem, for I will send you far away to the Gentiles!"

The crowd listened until Paul came to that word; then with one voice they shouted, "Kill him! He isn't fit to live!" The commander brought Paul inside and ordered him lashed with whips to make him confess his crime. As they tied Paul down to lash him, Paul said to the officer, "Is it legal for you to whip a Roman citizen who hasn't even been tried?"

The soldiers who were about to interrogate Paul quickly withdrew when they heard he was a Roman citizen. The next day the commander freed Paul from his chains and ordered the leading priests into session with the Jewish high council. He had Paul brought in before them.

Gazing at the high council, Paul began: "Brothers, I have always lived before God in all good conscience!" Ananias the high priest commanded those close to Paul to slap him but Paul said to him, "God will slap you, you whitewashed wall! What kind of judge are you to break the law yourself by ordering me struck like that?" Those standing near Paul said to him, "Is that the way to talk to God's high priest?" "I'm sorry, brothers. I didn't realize he was the high priest."

Paul realized that some members of the high council were Sadducees and some were Pharisees, so he shouted, "Brothers, I am a Pharisee! I am on trial because my hope is in the resurrection of the dead!"

This divided the council for the Sadducees say there is no resurrection or angels or spirits but the Pharisees believe in all of these. A great clamor arose and the commander ordered his soldiers to take him back to the fortress. That night the Lord appeared to Paul and said, "Be encouraged, Paul. Just as you have told the people about me here in Jerusalem, you must preach the Good News in Rome."

The next morning a group of Jews went to the leading priests and other leaders and told them "We have bound ourselves under oath to neither eat nor drink until we have killed Paul." Paul's nephew heard of their plan and went to the fortress and told Paul. Paul called one of the officers and said, "Take this young man to the commander. Paul's nephew told him, "Some Jews are going to ask you to bring Paul before the Jewish high council tomorrow. There are more than forty men hiding along the way ready to kill him."

The commander called two of his officers and ordered, "Get two hundred soldiers ready to leave for Caesarea at nine o'clock tonight. Take two hundred spearmen and seventy horsemen. Provide horses for Paul and get him safely to Governor Felix."

Paul's imprisonment in Caesarea[32]

When they arrived in Caesarea they presented Paul to Governor Felix. [33] "I will hear your case myself when your accusers arrive," the governor told him. The governor ordered him kept in the prison at Herod's headquarters.

---

32 From Acts 24-26.

33 Historical Background: Felix, the Roman governor, ruled with an iron fist. Once an Egyptian Jew led a small army of followers to the Mount of Olives, just across from the Jewish Temple in Jerusalem, promising to make the Jerusalem walls fall down. Felix sent soldiers to intervene and although the Egyptian escaped, hundreds of his followers were killed. Later, when violence broke out in Caesarea Felix sent in troops who massacred the people and then even looted their homes! Felix was married to a Jewish woman named Drusilla. She was the sister of Herod Agrippa II and was known for her great beauty. Drusilla first got married when she was only sixteen but while still in her teens, she met Felix who persuaded her to leave her husband to marry him. He had already been married twice before. Paul was still imprisoned in Caesarea when Felix was removed from office because of the massacre in Caesarea. Felix was replaced with Porcius Festus who governed as procurator of Judea from AD 59-62. Stott, 363; cf. also Hemer, Colin. The Book of Acts in the Setting of Hellenistic History. Winona Lake, IN : Eisenbrauns, 1990, 130, 172-173, 254.

Five days later Ananias, the high priest, arrived with some of the Jewish leaders and the lawyer Tertullus. Tertullus laid charges against Paul. Paul said, I didn't argue with anyone in the Temple nor did I incite a riot in any synagogue or on the streets of the city. But I admit that I follow the Way, which they call a sect. I worship the God of our ancestors and I firmly believe the Jewish law and everything written in the books of prophecy. My accusers saw me in the Temple as I was completing a purification ritual. There was no crowd around me and no rioting. Ask these men here what wrongdoing the Jewish high council found in me, except for one thing I said when I shouted out, I am on trial before you today because I believe in the resurrection of the dead!

Felix, who was quite familiar with the Way, adjourned the hearing and said, "Wait until Lysias, the garrison commander, arrives. Then I will decide the case." He ordered an officer to keep Paul in custody but to give him some freedom and allow his friends to visit him and take care of his needs.

A few days later Felix came with his wife, Drusilla, who was Jewish. Sending for Paul, they listened as he told them about faith in Christ Jesus. As he reasoned with them about righteousness and self-control and the judgment to come, Felix was terrified. "Go away for now," he replied. "When it is more convenient, I'll call for you again." He hoped that Paul would bribe him so he sent for him quite often and talked with him. Two years went by in this way; then Felix was succeeded by Porcius Festus. Because Felix wanted to gain favor with the Jewish leaders, he left Paul in prison.

Three days after Festus arrived in Caesarea to take over his new responsibilities he left for Jerusalem where the leading priests and other Jewish leaders made their accusations against Paul. They asked Festus to transfer Paul to Jerusalem (Their plan was to kill him). Festus replied that Paul was at Caesarea and he himself would be returning there soon.

Eight or ten days later he returned to Caesarea and on the following day Paul's trial began. Jewish leaders from Jerusalem made many serious accusations they couldn't prove. Paul denied the charges. "I am not guilty," he said. "I have committed no crime against the Jewish laws or the Temple or the Roman government."

Festus, wanting to please the Jews, asked him, "Are you willing to go to Jerusalem and stand trial before me there?" Paul replied,

No! You know very well I am not guilty. If I have done something worthy of death, I don't refuse to die. But if I am innocent, neither you nor anyone else has a right to turn me over to these men to kill me. I appeal to Caesar!

Festus conferred with his advisers and then replied, "Very well! You have appealed to Caesar, and to Caesar you shall go!"

A few days later King Agrippa arrived with his sister, Bernice, to pay their respects to Festus. During their stay of several days, Festus discussed Paul's case with the king. "I'd like to hear the man myself," Agrippa said.

The next day Agrippa[34] and Bernice arrived at the auditorium with great pomp, accompanied by military officers and prominent men of the city. Festus ordered that Paul be brought in. Festus said, "King Agrippa and all present, this is the man whose death is demanded both by the local Jews and by those in Jerusalem. In my opinion he has done

34   The "King Agrippa" in the story above is Herod Agrippa II, the son of Herod Agrippa I. When the Book of Acts was written, many people would have easily understood the difference without explanation, just as informed people today understand that America has had two Presidents named Bush. Herod Agrippa II was only seventeen when his father died. Rome didn't think he was ready to rule Judea so they gave him a small kingdom in part of what is now Lebanon. Judea went back to being governed by procurators like Festus. Agrippa II and his sister, with whom he was rumored to be having an incestuous relationship, were apparently just paying respects to Festus, the new procurator. (Stott, 368; cf. Hemer, 173).

nothing worthy of death, however, he appealed his case to the emperor and I decided to send him."

Then Agrippa said to Paul, "You may speak in your defense." So Paul started his defense:

I am fortunate, King Agrippa, that you are the one hearing my defense against all these accusations, for I know you are an expert on Jewish customs and controversies. I was given a thorough Jewish training from my earliest childhood. I have been a member of the Pharisees. Authorized by the leading priests, I caused many of the believers in Jerusalem to be sent to prison and I cast my vote against them when they were condemned to death. Many times I had them whipped in the synagogues to try to get them to curse Christ. I was so violently opposed to them that I even hounded them in distant cities. One day I was on such a mission to Damascus. About noon, a light from heaven brighter than the sun shone down on me and my companions. We all fell down and I heard a voice saying to me in Aramaic, "Saul, Saul, why are you persecuting me?" Who are you, sir?' I asked. "I am Jesus, the one you are persecuting. I am going to send you to the Gentiles. They will receive forgiveness for their sins and be given a place among God's people who are set apart by faith in me. King Agrippa, I was not disobedient to that vision. I preached first to those in Damascus, then in Jerusalem and throughout all Judea, and also to the Gentiles, that all must turn from their sins and turn to God, and prove they have changed by the good things they do. Some Jews arrested me in the Temple for preaching this. They tried to kill me, but God protected me. I teach nothing except what the prophets and Moses said would happen, that the Messiah would suffer and be the first to rise from the dead as a light to Jews and Gentiles alike.

Suddenly Festus shouted, "Paul, you are insane. Too much study has made you crazy!"

Paul replied, I am not insane, Most Excellent Festus. I am speaking the sober truth. King Agrippa knows about these things. I speak frankly for I am sure these events are all familiar to him!

Then the king, the governor, Bernice, and all the others stood and left. As they talked it over they agreed, "This man hasn't done anything worthy of death or imprisonment." Agrippa said to Festus, "He could be set free if he hadn't appealed to Caesar!" [35]

Paul's voyage to Rome[36]

When the time came we set sail for Italy. Paul and several other prisoners were placed in the custody of an army officer named Julius, a captain of the Imperial Regiment. Aristarchus, a Macedonian from Thessalonica, was also with us. The next day we docked at Sidon. Julius was very kind to Paul and let him go ashore to visit with friends so they could provide for his needs.

Putting out to sea from there we encountered headwinds that made it difficult to keep the ship on course. We passed along the coast of the provinces of Cilicia and Pamphylia, landing at Myra. There the officer found an Egyptian ship from Alexandria that was bound for Italy and he put us on board. We had several days of rough sailing and after great difficulty we finally arrived at Fair Havens. The weather was becoming dangerous for long voyages by then because it was so late in the fall and Paul spoke to the ship's officers about it. "Sirs," he said, "I believe there is trouble ahead if we go on, shipwreck and danger to our lives." But the officer in charge of the prisoners listened more to the ship's

35   Meanwhile, in AD 58 back in Rome, Nero had his wife Octavia murdered so he could marry Poppea Sabina, the wife of a long-time drinking buddy. Nero's new wife convinced him to kill his mother. Nero arranged for the ship on which his mother was traveling, to have an "accident" while at sea. The ship sank but Nero's mother grabbed on to some wood and somehow managed to get back alive. Nero nearly fainted when he saw her, but he had her executed with a sword shortly thereafter. Nero then spread word it was her who tried to kill him! (Klingaman, 281).

36   From Acts 27-28.

captain and the owner than to Paul.

Since Fair Havens was an exposed harbor, a poor place to spend the winter, most of the crew wanted to go to Phoenix, farther up the coast of Crete, and spend the winter there. But the weather changed abruptly and a wind of typhoon strength caught the ship and blew it out to sea. The next day, as gale-force winds continued to batter the ship, the crew began throwing the cargo overboard. The following day they even threw out the ship's equipment and anything else they could lay their hands on. The terrible storm raged unabated for many days, blotting out the sun and the stars until at last all hope was gone.

Finally, Paul said, "Men, you should have listened to me and not left Fair Havens. But take courage! None of you will lose your lives. Last night an angel of the God whom I serve stood beside me and said, 'Don't be afraid, Paul, for you will surely stand trial before Caesar!' So take courage! I believe God. It will be just as he said. But we will be shipwrecked on an island."

About midnight on the fourteenth night of the storm the sailors took soundings and found the water was only 120 feet deep. A little later they sounded again and found only 90 feet. At this rate they were afraid we would soon be driven against the rocks along the shore so they threw out four anchors.

As the darkness gave way to the early morning light, Paul took some bread, gave thanks to God before them all, and broke off a piece and ate it. Then everyone was encouraged and all 276 of us began eating, for that is the number we had aboard. After eating, the crew lightened the ship further by throwing the cargo of wheat overboard.

When morning dawned they saw a bay with a beach and headed toward shore. The ship ran aground. The bow stuck fast while the stern was smashed by the force of the waves and began to break apart.

The soldiers wanted to kill the prisoners to make sure they didn't escape but the commanding officer wanted to spare Paul so he didn't let them carry out their plan. He ordered all who could swim to jump overboard and make for land and he told the others to try for it on planks and debris from the broken ship. Everyone escaped safely ashore!

We learned that we were on the island of Malta. The people were very kind to us. It was cold and rainy so they built a fire on the shore to warm us. As Paul gathered an armful of sticks and was laying them on the fire, a poisonous snake fastened itself onto his hand, but Paul shook off the snake into the fire and was unharmed. The people waited for him to swell up or suddenly drop dead. When they had waited a long time and saw no harm come to him, they decided he was a god.

Near the shore where we landed was an estate belonging to Publius, the chief official of the island. He welcomed us courteously and fed us for three days. As it happened, Publius's father was ill with fever and dysentery. Paul prayed for him, and laying his hands on him, he healed him. Then other sick people on the island came and were cured. As a result we were showered with honors, and when the time came to sail, people put on board all sorts of things we would need for the trip.

Three months after the shipwreck we set sail on another ship that had wintered at the island. Our first stop was Syracuse where we stayed three days. From there we sailed across to Rhegium. A day later a south wind began blowing so the following day we sailed up the coast to Puteoli. There we found some believers who invited us to stay with them seven days. And so we came to Rome.[37]

---

37   By the time Paul got to Rome in AD 60, Nero was devoting a considerable amount of time to acting. He produced performances known as "Juvenalia" in which the sons and daughters of Roman aristocrats were forced to take part in pornographic plays and athletic contests. Technology changes, but human nature was as sinful in

Paul's imprisonment in Rome[38]

When we arrived in Rome, Paul was permitted to have his own private lodging, though he was guarded by a soldier. Three days after Paul's arrival, he called together the local Jewish leaders. He said to them,

Brothers, I was arrested in Jerusalem and handed over to the Roman government even though I had done nothing against our people or the customs of our ancestors. The Romans tried me and wanted to release me but when the Jewish leaders protested the decision, I felt it necessary to appeal to Caesar. I asked you to come here today so I could tell you that I am bound with this chain because I believe that the hope of Israel, the Messiah, has already come.

They replied, "We have heard nothing against you, but we want to hear what you believe for the only thing we know about these Christians is that they are denounced everywhere."

A time was set, and on that day a large number of people came to Paul's house. He taught them about Jesus from the Scriptures, from the five books of Moses and the books of the prophets. He began lecturing in the morning and went on into the evening. Some believed and some didn't. But after they had argued back and forth among themselves, they left with this final word from Paul:

The Holy Spirit was right when he said through Isaiah the prophet, 'Go and say to my people, 'You will hear my words but you will not understand; you will see what I do but you will not perceive its meaning. The hearts of these people are hardened, their ears cannot hear, they have closed their eyes and their hearts cannot understand.' This salvation from God is also available to the Gentiles and they will accept it.

For the next two years Paul lived in his own rented house. He welcomed all who visited him, proclaiming the

Paul's time as it is in our own (Klingaman, 292-301).
38   From Acts 28.

Kingdom of God with all boldness and teaching about the Lord Jesus Christ. And no one tried to stop him.

Historical Background

The Book of Acts ends in AD 62 with Paul under house arrest in Rome. We are not told what happened to him. Later accounts suggest that he may have been released and that he may have even ministered in Spain, though it is not certain how reliable these reports are.

While Paul was under arrest in Rome from AD 60-62, the situation in Judea was rapidly disintegrating into anarchy. A group of urban terrorists, called Sicarii, would hide in plain view in the crowds of Jerusalem, stab their victims and blend in with the crowds. In AD 62 the same Festus who had kept Paul under arrest in Caesarea, had James, the leader of the Jerusalem church and half brother of Jesus executed.

A mild form of Roman imprisonment was house arrest in which the prisoner could stay in his own house accompanied by a guard. From AD 60-62, Paul wrote what we now call "The Prison Epistles," Ephesians, Philippians, Colossians and Philemon.

CHAPTER SEVEN

Paul's Prison Letters: Ephesians

Introduction to Ephesians

Some scholars have noted that Paul's letter to the Ephesians sounds like it was written to a church Paul had never visited, not to a church like Ephesus where he ministered for so long. Since some ancient manuscripts of Ephesians do not contain the address "to Ephesus," some scholars speculate that this letter may have originally been Paul's letter to the church in nearby Laodicea.

In other words, what you read below is Paul's letter to the Ephesians, but some speculate (the key word is "speculate") that it may actually be a copy of a letter that Paul first sent to the Laodiceans. When Paul wrote to the church in Colossae (which is near Ephesus), he told them to share their letter with the Laodiceans and said that the Laodiceans should share the letter he sent to them also (Colossians 4:16). It may be that the Laodiceans also shared their letter with the Ephesians, as Paul would have wanted.

Whether the letter was originally addressed to Laodicea or to Ephesus is really irrelevant. Either way, the letter is from Paul and the essence of this letter appears below. The first part covers our amazing blessings in Christ, and the last half tells how we should then live in light of those blessings.

From Paul, chosen by God to be an apostle of Christ Jesus, to God's people in Ephesus who are faithful followers of Christ Jesus. May grace and peace be yours from God our Father and Jesus Christ our Lord.

How we praise God, the Father of our Lord Jesus Christ, who has blessed us with every spiritual blessing in the heavenly realms because we belong to Christ. Even before he made the world, God loved us and chose us in Christ to be holy and without fault in his eyes. His unchanging plan has always been to adopt us into his own family by bringing us to himself through Jesus Christ.

He purchased our freedom through the blood of his Son, and our sins are forgiven. God's plan has now been revealed to us, a plan centered on Christ: At the right time he will bring everything together under the authority of Christ, everything in heaven and on earth.

Furthermore, because of Christ, we have received an inheritance from God, for he chose us from the beginning. God's purpose was that we who were the first to trust in Christ should praise our glorious God. When you believed in Christ, he identified you as his own by giving you the Holy Spirit, whom he promised long ago. The Spirit is God's guarantee that he will give us everything he promised and that he has purchased us to be his own people. This is just one more reason for us to praise our glorious God.

I pray for you constantly, asking God, to give you spiritual wisdom and understanding, so that you might grow in your knowledge of God. I want you to realize what a rich and glorious inheritance he has given to his people. I pray that you will begin to understand the incredible greatness of his power for us who believe him, the same mighty power that raised Christ from the dead and seated him in the place of honor at God's right hand. God has put all things under the authority of Christ for the benefit of the church, his body.

Once you were dead, doomed forever because of your

many sins. You used to live just like the rest of the world, full of sin, obeying Satan. He is at work in the hearts of those who refuse to obey God. All of us used to live that way, following the passions and desires of our evil nature. We were born with an evil nature and we were under God's anger just like everyone else.

But God loved us so very much that even while we were dead because of our sins, he gave us life when he raised Christ from the dead (It is only by God's special favor that you have been saved). God saved you by his special favor when you believed. You can't take credit for this; it is a gift from God. Salvation is not a reward for the good things we have done, so none of us can boast about it. He has created us anew in Christ Jesus so that we can do the good things he planned for us long ago.

Don't forget that you Gentiles used to be outsiders by birth. In those days you were living apart from Christ. You were excluded from God's people, Israel, and you did not know the promises God had made to them. But though you once were far away from God, now you have been brought near to him because of the blood of Christ.

Christ himself has made peace between us Jews and you Gentiles by making us all one people. By his death he ended the system of Jewish law that excluded the Gentiles. His purpose was to make peace between Jews and Gentiles by creating in himself one new person from the two groups. Together as one body, Christ reconciled both groups to God by means of his death.

He has brought this Good News of peace to you Gentiles who were far away from him, and to us Jews who were near. Now both Jews and Gentiles may come to the Father through the same Holy Spirit because of what Christ has done for us. Now you Gentiles are no longer strangers and foreigners. You are citizens along with all of God's holy people. You are members of God's family. We are his house, built on the foundation of the apostles and the prophets, and the cornerstone is Christ Jesus himself.

I, Paul, am a prisoner of Christ Jesus because of my preaching to you Gentiles. As you already know, God has given me this ministry of announcing his favor to you Gentiles. God did not reveal it to previous generations, but now he has revealed it by the Holy Spirit to his holy apostles and prophets. This is the plan: The Gentiles have an equal share with the Jews in all the riches inherited by God's children. Both groups have believed the Good News and both are part of the same body and enjoy together the promise of blessings through Christ Jesus.

Just think! Though I did nothing to deserve it, and though I am the least deserving Christian, I was chosen to explain to everyone this plan that God had kept secret from the beginning. Because of Christ and our faith in him, we can now come fearlessly into God's presence, assured of his glad welcome. So please don't despair because of what they are doing to me here.

When I think of the wisdom of God's plan, I pray that he will give you mighty inner strength through his Holy Spirit. May your roots go down deep into the soil of God's marvelous love and may you have the power to understand how wide, how long, how high, and how deep his love really is. May you experience the love of Christ, though it is so great you will never fully understand it.

Glory be to God! By his mighty power at work within us, he is able to accomplish infinitely more than we would ever dare to ask or hope. May he be given glory in the church and in Christ Jesus forever and ever through endless ages.

Therefore I, a prisoner for serving the Lord, beg you to lead a life worthy of your calling. Be humble and gentle. Be patient with each other, making allowance for each other's faults. Always keep yourselves united in the Holy Spirit and bind yourselves together with peace.

We are all one body, we have the same Spirit, and we have all been called to the same glorious future. There is only one Lord, one faith, one baptism, and there is only one God and Father. However, he has given each one of us a special gift according to the generosity of Christ. He gave these gifts to the church: the apostles, the prophets, the evangelists, and the pastors and teachers. Their responsibility is to equip God's people to do his work and build up the church, the body of Christ, until we come to such unity in our faith and knowledge of God's Son that we will be mature and full grown in the Lord.

Then we will no longer be like children, forever changing our minds about what we believe because someone has told us something different or because someone has cleverly lied to us. Instead, we will hold to the truth in love, becoming more and more in every way like Christ, who is the head of his body, the church. Under his direction, the whole body is fitted together perfectly. As each part does its own special work, it helps the other parts grow, so that the whole body is healthy and growing and full of love.

With the Lord's authority let me say this: Live no longer as the ungodly do. Their closed minds are full of darkness; they are far away from the life of God because they have shut their minds and hardened their hearts against him. They have given themselves over to immoral ways. Their lives are filled with all kinds of impurity and greed.

That isn't what you were taught when you learned about Christ! Throw off your old evil nature and your former way of life, which is rotten through and through, full of lust and deception. Instead, there must be a spiritual renewal of your thoughts and attitudes. Display a new nature because you are a new person, created in God's likeness, righteous, holy, and true.

So put away all falsehood and "tell your neighbor the truth." And "don't sin by letting anger gain control over you."

Don't let the sun go down while you are still angry, for anger gives a mighty foothold to the Devil. If you are a thief, stop stealing. Begin using your hands for honest work, and then give generously to others in need.

Don't use foul or abusive language. Let everything you say be good and helpful so that your words will be an encouragement to those who hear them. Do not bring sorrow to God's Holy Spirit by the way you live. Get rid of all bitterness, rage, anger, harsh words, and slander, as well as all types of malicious behavior. Instead, be kind to each other, tenderhearted, forgiving one another, just as God through Christ has forgiven you.

Live a life filled with love for others, following the example of Christ, who loved you and gave himself as a sacrifice to take away your sins. Let there be no sexual immorality, impurity, or greed among you. Obscene stories, foolish talk, and coarse jokes are not for you. Instead, let there be thankfulness to God. You can be sure that no immoral, impure, or greedy person will inherit the Kingdom of Christ and of God, for a greedy person is really an idolater who worships the things of this world.

Don't be fooled by those who try to excuse these sins, for the terrible anger of God comes upon all those who disobey him. Take no part in the worthless deeds of evil and darkness; instead, rebuke and expose them. It is shameful even to talk about the things that ungodly people do in secret. Where your light shines, it will expose their evil deeds.

So be careful how you live, not as fools but as those who are wise. Make the most of every opportunity for doing good in these evil days. Don't act thoughtlessly but try to understand what the Lord wants you to do. Don't be drunk with wine, instead let the Spirit fill you, making music to the Lord in your hearts. Always give thanks for everything to God the Father in the name of our Lord Jesus Christ.

Submit to one another out of reverence for Christ. Wives submit to your husbands as you do to the Lord. A husband is the head of his wife as Christ is the head of his body, the church; he gave his life to be her Savior. As the church submits to Christ, so wives must submit to your husbands.

Husbands love your wives with the same love Christ showed the church. He gave his life for her to make her holy and clean, washed by baptism and God's word. In the same way, each man must love his wife as he loves himself, and the wife must respect her husband.

Children, obey your parents. "Honor your father and mother." This is the first of the Ten Commandments that ends with a promise. Fathers, don't make your children angry by the way you treat them. Rather, bring them up with the discipline and instruction approved by the Lord.

Slaves, obey your earthly masters with deep respect and fear. Serve them sincerely as you would serve Christ. Work hard, but not just to please your masters when they are watching. Masters must treat your slaves right. Don't threaten them; remember, you both have the same Master in heaven, and he has no favorites.

Be strong with the Lord's mighty power. Put on God's armor so that you will be able to stand firm against all strategies and tricks of the Devil. We are not fighting against people but against the evil rulers and authorities of the unseen world. Use God's armor to resist the enemy, so that after the battle you will still be standing firm.

Stand your ground, putting on the sturdy belt of truth and the body armor of God's righteousness. For shoes, put on the peace that comes from the Good News. You will need faith as your shield to stop the fiery arrows aimed at you by Satan. Put on salvation as your helmet, and take the sword of the Spirit, which is the word of God. Pray at all times in the power of the Holy Spirit. Stay alert and be persistent in your prayers for all Christians everywhere.

Pray for me, that I will keep on speaking boldly for him as I should. Tychicus, a faithful helper in the Lord's work, will tell you how I am getting along. May God's grace be upon all who love our Lord Jesus Christ with an undying love.

CHAPTER EIGHT

Paul's Prison Epistles: Philippians

Introduction to Philippians

While Paul was in prison in Rome, the church in Philippi sent a man named Epaphroditus with a love-gift for Paul. Even though he was in prison, Paul's letter to the Philippians is his most joyful letter. It is Paul's thank you letter for the gifts the Philippians had just sent

---

This letter is from Paul and Timothy, slaves of Christ Jesus, to all of God's people in Philippi. May God our Father and the Lord Jesus Christ give you grace and peace.

I always pray for you, and make my requests with a heart full of joy because you have been my partners in spreading the Good News from the time you first heard it until now. You have a very special place in my heart. We have shared together the blessings of God, both when I was in prison and when I was out, defending the truth and telling others the Good News.

I want you to know, brothers and sisters that everything that has happened to me here has helped to spread the Good News. Everyone here, including all the soldiers in the palace guard, knows that I am in chains because of Christ. Because of my imprisonment many of the Christians here have become more bold in telling others about Christ.

I know that as you pray for me and as the Spirit of Jesus Christ helps me, this will all turn out for my deliverance. I live in eager expectation and hope that I will always be bold for Christ and that my life will always honor Christ, whether I live or I die.

To me, living is for Christ and dying is even better. If I live, that means fruitful service for Christ. I'm torn between two desires: Sometimes I want to live, and sometimes I long to go and be with Christ. That would be far better for me, but it is better for you that I live.

Whatever happens to me, live in a manner worthy of the Good News about Christ as citizens of heaven. Don't be intimidated by your enemies for you have been given not only the privilege of trusting in Christ but also the privilege of suffering for him.

Is there any encouragement from belonging to Christ, any fellowship together in the Spirit? Then make me truly happy by loving one another and working together with one heart and purpose. Don't be selfish; don't live to make a good impression on others. Be humble, thinking of others as better than yourself. Don't think only about your own affairs but be interested in others too.

Your attitude should be the same that Christ Jesus had. Though he was God, he did not demand and cling to his rights as God. He made himself nothing; he took the humble position of a slave and appeared in human form. He obediently humbled himself even further by dying a criminal's death on a cross. Because of this, God raised him up to the heights of heaven and gave him a name that is above every other name, so that at the name of Jesus every knee will bow and every tongue will confess that Jesus Christ is Lord, to the glory of God the Father.

Stay away from complaining and arguing. Live clean, innocent lives as children of God in a dark world full of crooked and perverse people. Let your lives shine brightly before them. Even if my life is to be poured out like a drink offering to complete the sacrifice of your faithful service (that is, if I am to die for you), I will rejoice, and I want to share my joy with all of you.

If the Lord Jesus is willing, I hope to send Timothy to you soon. Then when he comes back, he can cheer me up by telling me how you are getting along. Like a son with his father, he has helped me in preaching the Good News. I hope to send him to you just as soon as I find out what is going to happen to me here.

Meanwhile, I thought I should send Epaphroditus back to you. He is a true brother, a faithful worker. He was your messenger to help me in my need. He was very distressed that you heard he was ill. In fact, he almost died. But God had mercy on him and also on me, so that I would not have such unbearable sorrow. Welcome him with Christian love and be sure to honor people like him for he risked his life for the work of Christ.

Whatever happens, brothers and sisters, may the Lord give you joy. Watch out for those dogs, those wicked men and their evil deeds, those mutilators who say you must be circumcised to be saved. We who worship God in the Spirit are the only ones who are truly circumcised. We put no confidence in human effort. Instead, we boast about what Christ Jesus has done for us

Yet I could have confidence in myself if anyone could. I was circumcised when I was eight days old, having been born into a pure-blooded Jewish family, of the tribe of Benjamin. I was a member of the Pharisees, who demand the strictest obedience to the Jewish law. And zealous? Yes, in fact, I harshly persecuted the church. I obeyed the Jewish law so carefully that I was never accused of any fault.

I once thought all these things were so very important but now I consider everything worthless when compared with the priceless gain of knowing Christ Jesus my Lord. I have discarded everything else, counting it all as garbage, so that I may have Christ and become one with him.

I no longer count on my own goodness or my ability to obey God's law, but I trust Christ to save me. God's way of making us right with himself depends on faith. As a result, I can really know Christ and experience the mighty power that raised him from the dead. I can learn what it means to suffer with him, sharing in his death, so that, somehow, I can experience the resurrection from the dead!

I don't mean to say that I have already reached perfection but I am focusing all my energies on this one thing: Forgetting the past and looking forward to what lies ahead, I strain to reach the end of the race and receive the prize for which God, through Christ Jesus, is calling us up to heaven.

Brothers and sisters pattern your lives after mine and learn from those who follow our example. I say again with tears in my eyes, that there are many whose conduct shows they are really enemies of the cross of Christ. Their future is eternal destruction. Their god is their appetite, they brag about shameful things and all they think about is this life here on earth.

But we are citizens of heaven where the Lord Jesus Christ lives and we are eagerly waiting for him to return as our Savior. He will take these weak mortal bodies of ours and change them into glorious bodies like his own. Brothers and sisters, I love you and long to see you, so please stay true to the Lord.

Now I want to plead with Euodia and Syntyche. Please settle your disagreement. I ask you, my true teammate, to help these women, for they worked hard with me in telling others the Good News. They worked with Clement and the rest of my co-workers, whose names are written in the Book of Life.

Always be full of joy in the Lord. Rejoice! Let everyone

see that you are considerate in all you do. Remember, the Lord is coming soon. Don't worry about anything; instead, pray about everything. Tell God what you need and thank him for all he has done. If you do this you will experience God's peace which is far more wonderful than the human mind can understand. His peace will guard your hearts and minds as you live in Christ Jesus.

Now, fix your thoughts on what is true and honorable and right. Think about things that are pure and lovely and admirable, things that are excellent and worthy of praise.

I have learned how to get along happily whether I have much or little. I have learned the secret of living in every situation, whether it is with a full stomach or empty, with plenty or little. For I can do everything with the help of Christ who gives me the strength I need.

Even so, you have done well to share with me in my present difficulty. As you know, you Philippians were the only ones who gave me financial help when I brought you the Good News and then traveled on from Macedonia. No other church did this.

Even when I was in Thessalonica you sent help more than once. At the moment I have all I need! I am generously supplied with the gifts you sent with Epaphroditus. This same God who takes care of me will supply all your needs from his glorious riches which have been given to us in Christ Jesus.

Now glory be to God our Father forever and ever. Give my greetings to all the Christians there. The brothers who are with me here send you their greetings, especially those who work in Caesar's palace. May the grace of the Lord Jesus Christ be with your spirit.

CHAPTER NINE

Paul's Prison Letters: Colossians and Philemon

Introduction to Colossians

Colossians is directed to the church in Colossae, a city in the same general region as Ephesus. Epaphras, one of Paul's co-workers, told Paul about this church and Paul wrote his letter to the Colossians to help ground them in sound doctrine about Christ, to correct some false teaching to which they had been exposed, and to encourage them to live godly lives in Christ. Paul's co-workers, Tychicus and Onesimus were sent to deliver this letter. As we will see later, this same Onesimus is also the subject of Paul's letter to Philemon. The essence of Paul's letter to the Colossians appears below

---

From Paul, an apostle of Christ Jesus, and from our brother Timothy, to God's holy people in the city of Colossae. May God our Father give you grace and peace.

We always pray for you and give thanks to God the Father of our Lord Jesus Christ, for we have heard that you trust in Christ Jesus and that you love God's people. This same Good News is going out all over the world, changing lives everywhere, just as it changed yours. Epaphras, our co-worker was the one who brought you the Good News. He is the one who told us about the great love for others that the Holy Spirit has given you.

We ask God to give you a complete understanding of what he wants to do in your lives and to make you wise with spiritual wisdom. Then the way you live will always honor and please the Lord and you will continually do good, kind things for others. All the while, you will learn to know God better and better.

We also pray that you will be strengthened with his glorious power so that you will have all the patience and endurance you need. May you be filled with joy, always thanking the Father who has enabled you to share the inheritance that belongs to God's holy people. He has rescued us from the one who rules in the kingdom of darkness and has brought us into the Kingdom of his dear Son. God has purchased our freedom with his blood and has forgiven all our sins.

Christ is the visible image of the invisible God. He existed before God made anything and is supreme over all creation. Christ is the one through whom God created everything in heaven and earth. Everything has been created through him and for him and he holds all creation together. Christ is the head of the church which is his body. He is the first of all who will rise from the dead so he is first in everything.

God in all his fullness was pleased to live in Christ and by him God reconciled everything to himself. He made peace with everything in heaven and on earth by means of his blood on the cross. This includes you who were once so far away from God. You were his enemies, separated from him by your evil thoughts and actions, yet now he has brought you back as his friends. He has done this through his death on the cross in his own body. As a result, he has brought you into the very presence of God and you are holy and blameless as you stand before him without a single fault.

Continue to believe this truth and stand in it firmly. Don't drift away from the assurance you received when you heard the Good News. The Good News has been preached all over the world, and I, Paul, have been appointed by God to proclaim it. I am glad when I suffer for you in my body.

God has given me the responsibility of serving his church by proclaiming his message to you Gentiles. This message was kept secret for centuries but now it has been revealed for it has pleased God to tell his people that the riches and glory of Christ are for you Gentiles, too. This is the secret: Christ lives in you and this is your assurance that you will share in his glory.

Everywhere we go, we tell everyone about Christ. We warn them and teach them with all the wisdom God has given us, for we want to present them to God, perfect in their relationship to Christ. I work very hard at this, as I depend on Christ's mighty power that works within me.

I want you to know how much I have agonized for you and for the church at Laodicea, and for many other friends who have never known me personally. My goal is that they will be encouraged and knit together by strong ties of love. I want them to have full confidence because they have complete understanding of God's plan, which is Christ himself. In him lie hidden all the treasures of wisdom and knowledge. I am telling you this so that no one will be able to deceive you with persuasive arguments.

I am very happy because you are living as you should and because of your strong faith in Christ. Continue to live in obedience to him. Let your lives overflow with thanksgiving for all he has done. Don't let anyone lead you astray with empty philosophy and high-sounding nonsense that come from human thinking and from the evil powers of this world. In Christ the fullness of God lives in a human body and you are complete through your union with Christ. He is the Lord over every ruler and authority in the universe.

When you came to Christ you were "circumcised," but not by a physical procedure. It was a spiritual procedure, the cutting away of your sinful nature. You were buried with Christ when you were baptized and with him you were raised to a new life because you trusted the mighty power of God, who raised Christ from the dead.

You were dead because of your sins. Then God made you alive with Christ. He forgave all our sins. He canceled the record that contained the charges against us. He destroyed it by nailing it to Christ's cross. In this way God disarmed the evil rulers and authorities. He shamed them publicly by his victory over them on the cross of Christ.

Don't let anyone condemn you for what you eat or drink, or for not celebrating certain holy days or new-moon ceremonies or Sabbaths. These rules were only shadows of the real thing, Christ himself. Don't let anyone condemn you by insisting on self-denial and don't let anyone say you must worship angels, even though they say they have had visions about this.

These people claim to be so humble but their sinful minds have made them proud. They are not connected to Christ, the head of the body. You have died with Christ and he has set you free from the evil powers of this world. So why do you keep on following rules of the world, such as, "Don't handle, don't eat, don't touch." Such rules are mere human teaching. These rules may seem wise because they require strong devotion, humility, and severe bodily discipline, but they have no effect when it comes to conquering a person's evil thoughts and desires.

Since you have been raised to new life with Christ, set your sights on the realities of heaven where Christ sits at God's right hand in the place of honor and power. Let heaven fill your thoughts. Do not think only about things down here on earth. Have nothing to do with sexual sin, impurity, lust, and shameful desires. Don't be greedy for the good things of this life, for that is idolatry. God's terrible anger will come upon those who do such things.

But now is the time to get rid of anger, rage, malicious behavior, slander, and dirty language. Don't lie to each other, for you have stripped off your old evil nature and all its wicked deeds. In its place you have clothed yourselves with a new nature that is continually being renewed as you learn more and more about Christ, who created this new nature within you. In this new life, it doesn't matter if you are a Jew or a Gentile, circumcised or uncircumcised, barbaric, uncivilized, slave, or free. Christ is all that matters, and he lives in all of us.

Since God chose you to be the holy people whom he loves, clothe yourselves with tenderhearted mercy, kindness, humility, gentleness, and patience. Make allowance for each other's faults and forgive the person who offends you. Remember, the Lord forgave you, so you must forgive others.

Love is what binds us all together in perfect harmony. Let the peace that comes from Christ rule in your hearts and always be thankful. Let the words of Christ live in your hearts and make you wise. Use his words to teach and counsel each other. Sing psalms and hymns and spiritual songs to God with thankful hearts, and whatever you do or say, let it be as a representative of the Lord Jesus, all the while giving thanks through him to God the Father.

Wives, submit to your husbands, as is fitting for those who belong to the Lord. Husbands love your wives and never treat them harshly. Children obey your parents, for this is what pleases the Lord. Fathers, don't aggravate your children.

You slaves must obey your earthly masters willingly because of your reverent fear of the Lord. Work hard and cheerfully at whatever you do, as though you were working for the Lord. Remember that the Lord will give you an inheritance as your reward. But if you do what is wrong, you will be paid back for the wrong you have done. You slave owners must be just and fair to your slaves. Remember that you also have a Master in heaven.

Devote yourselves to prayer with an alert mind and

a thankful heart. Don't forget to pray for us, too, that God will give us many opportunities to preach about his plan that Christ is also for you Gentiles. That is why I am here in chains. Pray that I will proclaim this message as clearly as I should.

Live wisely among those who are not Christians and make the most of every opportunity. Let your conversation be gracious and effective so that you will have the right answer for everyone.

Tychicus, a much loved brother, will tell you how I am getting along. I am also sending Onesimus, a faithful and much loved brother, one of your own. He and Tychicus will give you all the latest news.

Aristarchus, who is in prison with me, sends you his greetings, and so does Mark, Barnabas's cousin. Make Mark welcome if he comes your way. Jesus (the one we call Justus) also sends his greetings.

Epaphras, from your city, a servant of Christ Jesus, sends you his greetings. He prays earnestly for you. Doctor Luke sends his greetings and so does Demas. Give my greetings to our Christian brothers and sisters at Laodicea and to Nympha and those who meet in her house.

After you have read this letter, pass it on to the church at Laodicea so they can read it, too and you should read the letter I wrote to them. Here is my greeting in my own handwriting, PAUL. Remember my chains. May the grace of God be with you.

Introduction to Philemon

Paul's letters to the Colossians and Philemon go together. Colossians is addressed to the church in Colossae while Paul's letter to Philemon is a personal letter directly to Philemon, a wealthy member of the Colossian church. Onesimus, one of Philemon's slaves, had run away and had later been saved under Paul's ministry in prison. Although Paul clearly wanted to keep Onesimus as a co-worker, Paul felt obligated to send him back, warning Philemon to treat him as if he were Paul

This letter is from Paul, in prison for preaching the Good News about Christ Jesus, and from our brother Timothy, to Philemon, our much loved co-worker, and to our sister Apphia and to Archippus, a fellow soldier of the cross. I am also writing to the church that meets in your house. May God our Father and the Lord Jesus Christ give you grace and peace.

I always thank God when I pray for you, Philemon, because I keep hearing of your trust in the Lord Jesus and your love for all of God's people. I myself have gained much joy and comfort from your love, my brother, because your kindness has so often refreshed the hearts of God's people.

That is why I am boldly asking a favor of you. I could demand it in the name of Christ because it is the right thing for you to do, but because of our love I prefer just to ask you. Take this as a request from your friend Paul, an old man, now in prison for the sake of Christ Jesus.

My plea is that you show kindness to Onesimus. I think of him as my own son because he became a believer as a result of my ministry here in prison.

I am sending him back to you.[39] *I really wanted to keep*

---

39   Some people in America, blindly following the contemporary

him here with me while I am in these chains for preaching the Good News but I didn't want to do anything without your consent. I didn't want you to help because you were forced to do it. Perhaps you could think of it this way: Onesimus ran away for a little while so you could have him back forever. He is no longer just a slave; he is a beloved brother, especially to me.

So if you consider me your partner, give him the same welcome you would give me if I were coming. If he has harmed you in any way or stolen anything from you, charge me for it. I, Paul, write this in my own handwriting: "I will repay it." (I won't mention that you owe me your very soul)!

Dear brother, please do me this favor for the Lord's sake. Give me this encouragement in Christ. I am confident as I write this letter that you will do what I ask and even more!

Please keep a guest room ready for me, for I am hoping that God will answer your prayers and let me return to you soon. Epaphras, my fellow prisoner in Christ Jesus, sends you his greetings, so do Mark, Aristarchus, Demas, and Luke, my co-workers. The grace of the Lord Jesus Christ be with your spirit.

---

culture of their day, once tried to justify slavery by appealing to Philemon and to the Old Testament. The attempt was misguided, if not evil. The Romans and the Jews of Old Testament times generally enslaved people who were criminals, debtors, or prisoners of war. There is nothing in the Bible that justifies ripping innocent people from their homes and families simply because of their skin color and the greed of wealthy land owners! In fact, in Paul's first letter to Timothy (below), Paul himself condemns slave trading! Other American Christians strongly opposed slavery since the New Testament demands love and compassion, and cries out against both racism and greed. In Britain, it was a Christian, William Wilberforce, whose efforts eventually brought an end to slavery.

CHAPTER TEN

Pastoral Epistles: Titus

Introduction to the Pastoral Epistles

The three letters that remain are known as the "Pastoral Epistles" or letters. They are called Pastoral Epistles because they are personal letters from Paul to Timothy and Titus instructing them how to pastor the churches for which they are responsible.

Many modern critics believe these letters were written by Paul's later followers. Irenaeus (2nd century AD), however, clearly believed that the Pastoral Epistles were written by Paul. Not only does Irenaeus believe that Paul wrote the Pastoral Epistles, he doesn't see any need to argue or defend the point because the entire church at that time knew that Paul wrote these letters.

Second Timothy appears to be Paul's final letter, probably written shortly before his execution under the Roman Emperor Nero sometime between AD 64 and 68

Paul's letter to Titus

From Paul, a slave of God and an apostle of Jesus Christ. I have been sent to bring faith to those God has chosen and to teach them the truth that shows them how to live godly lives. It is by the command of God our Savior that I have been trusted to do this work. To Titus, my true child in the faith that we share. May God the Father and Christ Jesus our Savior give you grace and peace.

I left you on the island of Crete so you could complete our work there and appoint elders in each town as I instructed you. An elder must be well thought of for his good life. He must be faithful to his wife, and his children must be believers who are not wild or rebellious. An elder must live a blameless life, not arrogant or quick-tempered; he must not be a heavy drinker, violent, or greedy for money. He must enjoy having guests in his home. He must live wisely and be fair. He must live a devout and disciplined life.

He must have a strong and steadfast belief in the trustworthy message he was taught; then he will be able to encourage others with right teaching and show those who oppose it where they are wrong. There are many who rebel against right teaching and deceive people, this is especially true of those who insist on circumcision for salvation. They must be silenced. By their wrong teaching they have already turned whole families away from the truth. Such people claim they know God but they deny him by the way they live. They are despicable and disobedient, worthless for doing anything good.

Promote the kind of living that reflects right teaching. Teach the older men to exercise self-control, to be worthy of respect, and to live wisely. They must have strong faith and be filled with love and patience.

Teach the older women to live in a way that is appropriate for someone serving the Lord, not speaking evil of others and not heavy drinkers. Instead, they should teach others what is good. Older women must train the younger women to love their husbands and their children, to live wisely and be pure, to take care of their homes, to do good and be submissive to their husbands.

In the same way, encourage the young men to live wisely. Be an example to them by doing good deeds. Let everything you do reflect the integrity and seriousness of your teaching.

Slaves must obey their masters and do their best to please them. They must not talk back or steal but they must show themselves to be entirely trustworthy and good. Then they will make the teaching about God our Savior attractive in every way.

For the grace of God has been revealed, bringing salvation to all people. We are instructed to turn from godless living and sinful pleasures. We should live in this evil world with self-control, right conduct and devotion to God while we look forward to when the glory of our great God and Savior, Jesus Christ, will be revealed. He gave his life to free us from every kind of sin and to make us his own people, totally committed to doing what is right.

Teach these things and encourage your people to do them, correcting them when necessary. You have the authority to do this, so don't let anyone ignore you or disregard what you say.

Remind your people to submit to the government and its officers. They must not speak evil of anyone and they must avoid quarreling. Instead, they should be gentle and show true humility. Once we too were foolish and disobedient, but then God our Savior saved us, not because of the good things we did but because of his mercy. He washed away our sins and gave us a new life through the Holy Spirit. He declared us not guilty because of his great kindness.

Do not get involved in foolish discussions about spiritual pedigrees or in quarrels and fights about obedience to Jewish laws. If anyone is causing divisions among you, give a first and second warning. After that, have nothing more to do with that person for people like that have turned away from the truth. They are sinning and condemn themselves.

I am planning to send either Artemas or Tychicus to you. As soon as one of them arrives do your best to meet me at Nicopolis as quickly as you can, for I have decided to stay there for the winter. Do everything you can to help Zenas the lawyer and Apollos with their trip. Everybody here sends greetings. Please give my greetings to all of the believers who love us. May God's grace be with you all.

CHAPTER ELEVEN

Pastoral Epistles: First Timothy

From Paul, an apostle of Christ Jesus, appointed by the command of God our Savior and by Christ Jesus our hope, to Timothy, my true child in the faith. May God our Father and Christ Jesus our Lord give you grace, mercy, and peace.

When I left for Macedonia, I urged you to stay there in Ephesus and stop those who are teaching wrong doctrine. Don't let people waste time in endless speculation over myths and spiritual pedigrees. These things only cause arguments; they don't help people live a life of faith in God.

The purpose of my instruction is that all the Christians there would be filled with love that comes from a pure heart, a clear conscience, and sincere faith. Some teachers have turned away from these things and spend their time arguing and talking foolishness. They want to be known as teachers of the Law of Moses but they don't know what they are talking about.

We know these laws are good when they are used as God intended, but they were not made for people who do what is right. They are for people who are rebellious, ungodly and sinful, who consider nothing sacred, who murder, who are sexually immoral, for homosexuals and slave traders, for liars and oath breakers, and for those who do anything else that contradicts the right teaching.

How thankful I am to Christ Jesus our Lord for

appointing me to serve him, even though I used to scoff at the name of Christ. I hunted down his people, harming them in every way I could, but God had mercy on me because I did it in ignorance and unbelief.

Oh, how kind and gracious the Lord was! Christ Jesus came into the world to save sinners, and I was the worst of them all. But God had mercy on me so that Christ Jesus could use me as a prime example of his great patience with even the worst sinners. Then others will realize that they too, can believe in him and receive eternal life.

Timothy, my son, here are my instructions for you, based on the prophetic words spoken about you earlier. Cling tightly to your faith in Christ and always keep your conscience clear. Some people have deliberately violated their consciences; as a result, their faith has been shipwrecked. Hymenaeus and Alexander are two examples of this. I turned them over to Satan so they would learn not to blaspheme God.

I urge you to pray for all people. Plead for God's mercy upon them. Pray for kings and all others who are in authority so we can live in peace and quietness, in godliness and dignity. This pleases God our Savior for he wants everyone to be saved and to understand the truth. There is only one God and one Mediator who can reconcile God and people, the man Christ Jesus. He gave his life to purchase freedom for everyone and I have been chosen as a preacher and apostle to teach the Gentiles about faith and truth. So wherever you assemble, I want men to pray with holy hands lifted up to God, free from anger and controversy.

I want women to be modest in their appearance. They should wear decent and appropriate clothing and not draw attention to themselves by the way they fix their hair or by wearing gold or pearls or expensive clothes. Women who claim to be devoted to God should make themselves attractive by the good things they do. Women should listen and learn quietly and submissively. I do not let women teach men or have authority over them.

If someone wants to be an elder, he desires an honorable responsibility. An elder must be a man whose life cannot be spoken against. He must be faithful to his wife, exhibit self-control, live wisely and have a good reputation. He must enjoy having guests in his home and must be able to teach. He must not be a heavy drinker or violent. He must be gentle, peace loving, and not one who loves money. He must manage his own family well with children who respect and obey him. An elder must not be a new Christian. People outside the church must speak well of him.

Deacons must be people who are respected and have integrity. They must not be heavy drinkers and must not be greedy for money. They must be committed to the revealed truths of the Christian faith and must live with a clear conscience. Before they are appointed as deacons they should be given other responsibilities in the church as a test of their character and ability. If they do well then they may serve as deacons.

In the same way, their wives must be respected and must not speak evil of others. They must exercise self-control and be faithful in everything they do. A deacon must be faithful to his wife and he must manage his children and household well.

I am writing these things so that if I can't come for a while you will know how people must conduct themselves in the household of God.

This is the great mystery of our faith: Christ appeared in the flesh and was shown to be righteous by the Spirit. He was announced to the nations, believed on in the world, and was taken up into heaven.

Now the Holy Spirit tells us clearly that in the last times some will turn away from what we believe. They will follow lying spirits and teachings that come from demons.

These teachers are hypocrites and liars. They pretend to be religious but their consciences are dead. They will say it is wrong to be married and wrong to eat certain foods. But God created those foods to be eaten with thanksgiving by people who know and believe the truth.

Do not waste time arguing over godless ideas and old wives' tales. Spend your time and energy in training yourself for spiritual fitness. Physical exercise has some value but spiritual exercise is much more important for it promises a reward in both this life and the next.

We work hard and suffer much in order that people will believe the truth, for our hope is in the living God who is the Savior of all people, particularly of those who believe. Teach these things and insist that everyone learn them. Don't let anyone think less of you because you are young. Be an example to all believers in what you teach, in the way you live, in your love, your faith, and your purity.

Until I get there, focus on reading the Scriptures to the church, encouraging the believers, and teaching them. Do not neglect the spiritual gift you received through the prophecies spoken to you when the elders of the church laid their hands on you. Stay true to what is right and God will save you and those who hear you.

Never speak harshly to an older man but appeal to him respectfully as though he were your own father. Talk to the younger men as you would to your own brothers. Treat the older women as you would your mother and treat the younger women with all purity as your own sisters.

The church should care for any widow who has no one else to care for her. If she has children or grandchildren, their first responsibility is to show godliness at home and repay their parents by taking care of them. Those who won't care for their own relatives, especially those living in the same household, are worse than unbelievers.

A widow who is put on the list for support must be a woman who is at least sixty years old and was faithful to her husband. She must be well respected because of the good she has done. The younger widows should not be on the list because their physical desires will overpower their devotion to Christ and they will want to remarry. I advise these younger widows to marry again, have children, and take care of their own homes. If a Christian woman has relatives who are widows she must take care of them and not put the responsibility on the church.

Elders who do their work well should be paid well, especially those who work hard at both preaching and teaching. Do not listen to complaints against an elder unless there are two or three witnesses to accuse him. Anyone who sins should be rebuked in front of the whole church so that others will have a proper fear of God. I solemnly command you in the presence of God and Christ Jesus and the holy angels to obey these instructions without taking sides or showing special favor to anyone. Never be in a hurry about appointing an elder.

Do not participate in the sins of others. Keep yourself pure. Drink a little wine for the sake of your stomach because you are sick so often. Remember that some people lead sinful lives and will be judged. There are others whose sin will not be revealed until later. In the same way, everyone knows how much good some people do, but there are others whose good deeds won't be known until later.

Christians who are slaves should give their masters full respect so that the name of God and his teaching will not be shamed. If your master is a Christian, that is no excuse for being disrespectful. You should work all the harder because you are helping another believer by your efforts. Teach these truths, Timothy.

True religion with contentment is great wealth. After all, we didn't bring anything with us when we came into the world and we certainly cannot carry anything with us when we die. So if we have enough food and clothing, let us be content. But people who long to be rich fall into temptation. The love of money is at the root of all kinds of evil. Some people, craving money, have wandered from the faith and pierced themselves with many sorrows.

But you, Timothy, run from all these evil things and pursue a godly life, along with faith, love, perseverance, and gentleness. Fight the good fight for what we believe. Hold tightly to the eternal life that God has given you.

I command you before God and before Christ Jesus, who gave a good testimony before Pontius Pilate, that you obey his commands with all purity. At the right time Christ will be revealed from heaven by the blessed and only almighty God, the King of kings and Lord of lords.

Tell those who are rich in this world not to be proud and not to trust in their money which will soon be gone. Tell them to use their money to do good. They should be rich in good works and should give generously to those in need.

Timothy, guard what God has entrusted to you. Avoid godless, foolish discussions with those who oppose you with their so-called knowledge. Some people have wandered from the faith by following such foolishness. May God's grace be with you all.

CHAPTER TWELVE

Pastoral Epistles: Second Timothy

From Paul, an apostle of Christ Jesus, to Timothy, my dear son. May God our Father and Christ Jesus our Lord give you grace, mercy, and peace.

I thank God for you. Night and day I remember you in my prayers. I long to see you again for I remember your tears as we parted. I know that you sincerely trust the Lord for you have the faith of your mother, Eunice, and your grandmother, Lois.

This is why I remind you to fan into flames the spiritual gift God gave you when I laid my hands on you. God has not given us a spirit of fear and timidity but of power, love, and self-discipline. You must never be ashamed to tell others about our Lord, and don't be ashamed of me either, even though I'm in prison for Christ.

With the strength God gives you, be ready to suffer with me for the proclamation of the Good News. It is God who saved us and chose us to live a holy life. He did this not because we deserved it, but because that was his plan long before the world began, to show his love and kindness to us through Christ Jesus.

He has made all of this plain to us by the coming of Christ Jesus our Savior who broke the power of death and showed us the way to everlasting life through the Good News. God chose me to be a preacher, an apostle and a teacher of this Good News. That is why I am suffering here in prison but I am not ashamed of it for I know the one in whom I trust and I am sure that he is able to guard what I have entrusted to him until the day of his return.

Hold on to the pattern of right teaching you learned from me and remember to live in the faith and love that you have in Christ Jesus. With the help of the Holy Spirit who lives within us, carefully guard what has been entrusted to you.

As you know, the Christians who came here from the province of Asia have deserted me. May the Lord show special kindness to Onesiphorus and his family because he often visited and encouraged me. He was never ashamed of me because I was in prison. May the Lord show him special kindness on the day of Christ's return. You know how much he helped me at Ephesus.

Timothy, be strong with the special favor God gives you in Christ Jesus. You have heard me teach many things that have been confirmed by many reliable witnesses. Teach these great truths to trustworthy people who are able to pass them on to others. Endure suffering along with me as a good soldier of Christ Jesus. Do not let yourself become tied up in the affairs of this life for then you cannot satisfy the one who has enlisted you in his army.

Never forget that Jesus Christ was a man born into King David's family and that he was raised from the dead. Because I preach this Good News, I am suffering and have been chained like a criminal. But I am willing to endure anything if it will bring salvation and eternal glory in Christ Jesus to those God has chosen.

This is a true saying: If we die with him, we will also live with him. If we endure hardship, we will reign with him. If we deny him, he will deny us. If we are unfaithful, he remains faithful, for he cannot deny himself.

Remind everyone of these things. Be a good worker who does not need to be ashamed and who correctly explains the word of truth. Avoid godless, foolish discussions that lead *to more and more ungodliness. This kind of talk spreads like cancer.*

God's truth stands firm like a foundation stone with this inscription: "The Lord knows those who are his," and "Those who claim they belong to the Lord must turn away from all wickedness." In a wealthy home some utensils are made of gold and silver, and some are made of wood and clay. If you keep yourself pure, you will be a utensil God can use for his purpose.

Run from anything that stimulates youthful lust. Follow anything that makes you want to do right. Pursue faith, love and peace, and enjoy the companionship of those who call on the Lord with pure hearts. Again I say, don't get involved in foolish, ignorant arguments that only start fights. The Lord's servants must not quarrel but must be kind to everyone. They must be able to teach effectively and be patient with difficult people. They should gently teach those who oppose the truth.

You should also know this, Timothy, that the last days will be very difficult times. People will love only themselves and their money. They will be boastful and proud, scoffing at God, disobedient to their parents, and ungrateful. They will consider nothing sacred. They will be unloving and unforgiving; they will slander others and have no self-control; they will be cruel and have no interest in what is good. They will betray their friends, be reckless, be puffed up with pride, and love pleasure rather than God.

They will act as if they are religious but they will reject the power that could make them godly. Stay away from people like that. They are the kind who work their way into people's homes and win the confidence of vulnerable women who are burdened with the guilt of sin.

You know what I teach, how I live, and what my purpose in life is. You know my faith and how long I have suffered. You know my love and my patient endurance. You know how much persecution and suffering I have endured. You know all about how I was persecuted in Antioch, Iconium, and Lystra, but the Lord delivered me. Everyone who wants to live a godly life in Christ Jesus will suffer persecution.

Evil people and impostors will flourish. They will go on deceiving others and they themselves will be deceived. But you remain faithful to the things you have been taught. You know they are true for you know you can trust those who taught you. You have been taught the Holy Scriptures from childhood and they have given you the wisdom to receive the salvation that comes by trusting in Christ Jesus.

All Scripture is inspired by God and is useful to teach us what is true and to make us realize what is wrong in our lives. It straightens us out and teaches us to do what is right. It is God's way of preparing us in every way, fully equipped for every good thing God wants us to do.

I solemnly urge you before God and before Christ Jesus, who will someday judge the living and the dead when he appears to set up his Kingdom: Preach the word of God. Be persistent, whether the time is favorable or not. Patiently correct, rebuke, and encourage your people with good teaching. A time is coming when people will follow their own desires and will look for teachers who will tell them whatever they want to hear. They will reject the truth and follow strange myths.

Don't be afraid of suffering for the Lord. Work at bringing others to Christ. Complete the ministry God has given you. As for me, my life has already been poured out as an offering to God. The time of my death is near. I have fought a good fight, I have finished the race, and I have remained faithful. Now the prize awaits me, the crown of righteousness that the Lord, the righteous Judge, will give me on that great day of his return. The prize is not just for me but for all who eagerly look forward to his glorious return.

Please come as soon as you can. Demas has deserted

me because he loves the things of this life. Titus has gone to Dalmatia. Only Luke is with me. Bring Mark with you when you come for he will be helpful to me. I sent Tychicus to Ephesus. When you come, be sure to bring the coat I left with Carpus at Troas. Also bring my books and especially my papers.

The first time I was brought before the judge everyone had abandoned me. I hope it will not be counted against them. But the Lord stood with me and gave me strength that I might preach the Good News. He saved me from certain death. To God be the glory forever and ever.

Give my greetings to Priscilla and Aquila and those living at the household of Onesiphorus. Erastus stayed at Corinth, and I left Trophimus sick at Miletus. Hurry so you can get here before winter. Eubulus sends you greetings and so do Pudens, Linus, Claudia, and all the brothers and sisters. May the Lord be with your spirit. Grace be with you all.

APPENDIX ONE

After Paul

By AD 64 Nero had gone off the deep end! In his pubic performances he would have men and women tied to stakes while he dressed up in animal skins and attacked their genitals! During one performance an earthquake hit Rome but, unfortunately for his victims, Nero escaped.

Then a massive fire broke out in Rome, a city of over 700,000 inhabitants, many of whom lived in four or five story wooden apartment complexes. When rumors spread that Nero and his thugs were responsible for the fire, Nero blamed it on Christians! He had "immense multitudes" of Christians rounded up and tied to stakes to be attacked by animals or set on fire to illuminate his garden parties.

It is possible that both Peter and Paul were killed at this time. Tradition says that Peter was crucified. He asked to be crucified upside down because he didn't consider himself worthy to be crucified right side up as Jesus was. Paul, being a Roman citizen was exempt from crucifixion so he was beheaded. Meanwhile, back in Judea, the country had disintegrated into anarchy. In AD 62 Felix was succeeded by Gessius Florus. During a protest in Jerusalem, Florus responded by slaughtering 3,600 men, women and children. Wars and rebellions were breaking out all over the country and thousands were killed At one point,

Florus sent and army to Caesarea to put down one of the rebellions and killed 20,000 people!

The situation got so bad that the Romans sent an army from Syria to restore calm in Jerusalem, but Jerusalem fought back and killed 5,000 Roman soldiers, forcing them to retreat. When Nero heard of the defeat, he sent a veteran Roman general named Vespasian to put down the rebellions. By about AD 66, Vespasian's armies began marching through Galilee and Samaria destroying everyone who stood against him. All out war between Judea and Rome was underway!

Nero died in AD 68 and Vespasian went to claim the Roman throne. He left his son Titus whose armies had surrounded Jerusalem. They cut off all supplies to the city. After awhile, people inside the city ran out of food and were not only fighting each other for food, but they had divided into three warring factions and were killing each other! Because of so many dead bodies in the streets, pestilence was breaking out all over the city; people were dying from disease by the hundreds.

Finally, in AD 70, the Romans breached the walls of Jerusalem. Titus' men entered the holy place and destroyed the Temple just as Jesus had predicted some forty years earlier. Thousands were killed and thousands more were sent into slavery. Three years later, in AD 73, Masada, the last fortress fell and that was the end of the Jewish state—until it was resurrected in 1948.

As mentioned above, the book of Acts ends in AD 62. Scholars are not entirely sure when Paul was beheaded but it was probably between AD 64 and 68.

APPENDIX TWO

Paul's Letters and the New Testament Canon

It is becoming relatively common these days to hear or read of people who say that the New Testament was put together in the fourth century AD by powerful Christian bishops who only included the books that agreed with them and kicked all the others out. *The DaVinci Code* was an example of one book that makes that claim, but this nonsense is also being asserted by people who know better. The following are just a few ancient sources that show how Paul's letters were regarded, long before any Church council met to discuss the New Testament.

Second Peter

Roughly three hundred years before any church council met to discuss the issue of which books belonged to the New Testament (New Testament canon), Christians already viewed Paul's letters (and the Gospels too, for that matter) as sacred Scripture. In the little letter of Second Peter the author talks about "our beloved brother Paul" and says that the ignorant twist his letters just like they do with "the *other* Scriptures."[40]

Second Peter is a very controversial letter. Most Evangelicals believe Peter wrote it in the 60's AD. Most critics believe it was written by an unknown writer as late as 130 AD. Either way, this letter is an example of a very early Christian writer who classifies a collection of Paul's letters right up there with

---

40   Second Peter 3:15-16.

"the other Scriptures." Since the writer seems to see no need to argue his point, he is apparently knows that his readers will agree with him. In other words, he is not the only one who believes Paul's letters are Scripture.

Clement of Rome (AD 97)

Clement was a first century Christian leader in the church at Rome (he is often called "Clement of Rome" to distinguish him from a later Christian leader named "Clement of Alexandria"). Clement had personally conversed with the apostles themselves and it is even possible (more probable than not, in my view) that this Clement is the same Clement Paul mentions in Philippians 4:3.

Writing no later than AD 97, Clement clearly believed that Paul was writing "Scripture" under the inspiration of the Holy Spirit. Writing about Paul's letter that we call, First Corinthians, Clement says, "Take up the epistle of the blessed Apostle Paul...Truly, under the inspiration of the Spirit, he wrote to you concerning himself, and Cephas and Apollos."

Clement quotes from or alludes to Paul's writings several times in his letter, but he specifically cites First Corinthians 2:9 as Scripture and believes that the Scriptures are "the true utterances of the Holy Spirit."

In fact, according to Donald Hagner, Clement cites or alludes to the New Testament books of Matthew, Mark, Luke, John, Acts, Romans, 1 & 2 Corinthians, Galatians, Ephesians, Philippians, Colossians, 1 & 2 Timothy, Titus, Hebrews, James, 1 & 2 Peter, 1 John and Revelation.[41]

Clement is not just writing the personal opinions of a private

41   Hagner, Donald. *The Use of the Old and New Testaments in Clement of Rome.* Leiden : E.J. Brill, 1973, 351-352.

individual, but is expressing the beliefs of the church in his day.

Ignatius (AD 30-107)

Another prominent early Christian leader was a man named Ignatius who lived from AD 30-107. Ignatius was a Christian leader (actually a pastor to the pastors, like Clement) in Antioch. He was arrested for being a Christian and taken to Rome to stand trial. So committed was he to Jesus that he was willing, even eager, to be thrown to the lions for his faith.

Ignatius obviously had a very high view of Paul. To the Ephesians, Ignatius wrote,

"You are initiated into the mysteries of the Gospel with Paul, the holy, the martyred, the deservedly most happy, at whose feet may I be found, when I shall attain to God; who in all his Epistle makes mention of you in Christ Jesus."

Probably in case anyone might be tempted to view his own letters on the same level as those of Peter or Paul, Ignatius humbly acknowledges, "I do not, as Peter and Paul, issue commandments unto you. They were apostles...."

Throughout the letters of Ignatius, it is clear that Paul's letters, along with the Old Testament and the Gospels, are his authority. For all we know, Ignatius may have known all of Paul's letters but he quotes or alludes specifically to Romans, First Corinthians, Ephesians, Colossians, First and Second Timothy.

Polycarp AD 70-155

Yet another prominent leader in the early church was a man named Polycarp. He was arrested for being a Christian and given the choice to curse Jesus or die. Polycarp chose to die and was burned at the stake.

In about AD 110, Polycarp wrote a letter to the Philippians reminding them that Paul "accurately and steadfastly taught the word of truth" to them. Polycarp reminds the Philippians of the letter Paul wrote to them and says that if they carefully study it they would find it "to be the means of building you up in that faith...."

Polycarp writes, "For I trust that you are well versed in the sacred Scriptures...It is declared then in these Scriptures, 'Be angry, and sin not, and "Let not the sun go down on your wrath." This is a quote from Paul's letter to the Ephesians which Polycarp calls "Scripture." In addition to Ephesians and Philippians, Polycarp quotes or alludes to several of Paul's letters including, Romans, First and Second Corinthians, Galatians, First Thessalonians, First and Second Timothy.

Irenaeus (AD 194)

Irenaeus was a church leader in what we would now call France. In about AD 194 Irenaeus wrote *Against Heresies* to refute the numerous heresies flourishing in his day. In *Against Heresies*, Irenaeus called Peter and Paul "the most glorious apostles"[42] and clearly considered the "writings of the evangelists and apostles" to be Scripture.[43] For example he writes of the "forbidden deeds of which the Scriptures assures..." and what follows is a quote from Galatians 5:21.[44]

Irenaeus says this "tradition of the apostles" is "manifested throughout the whole word" and that the church can demonstrate a direct line of succession from the apostles to

42   Irenaeus. Against Heresies. III. 3. 2.
43   Irenaeus. Against Heresies. I. 3. 6; III. 12. 9.
44   Irenaeus. Against Heresies. I. 6. 3.

their successors down to Irenaeus' own time.[45] For example, Irenaeus writes of how Clement (discussed above) had personally seen and conversed with the apostles themselves.[46] Irenaeus writes of how Polycarp was "instructed by apostles" and "conversed with many who had seen Christ".[47] Irenaeus says Polycarp suffered martyrdom, "having always taught the things which he learned from the apostles.[48] Irenaeus says that when he was a young man, he heard Polycarp teaching.

In fact, even the heretics often acknowledged Paul's letters as Scripture. For example, Irenaeus charges Marcion (AD 140) with "mutilating the Scriptures," and "curtailing the Gospel according to Luke and the Epistles of Paul." Marcion was very anti-Jewish and while he accepted the Gospel of Luke and Paul's letters, he cut all the pro-Jewish material out to better fit his heresy.[49] Although many other heretics pretended to accept Paul's letters, Irenaeus charges them with taking Scripture out of context, twisting Scripture out of all recognition, mixing Scripture with other writings, and even fabricating their own Scriptures. For example, Irenaeus writes of the heretics:

> Such, then, is their system, which neither the prophets announced, nor the Lord taught, nor the apostles delivered, but of which they boast that beyond all others they have a perfect knowledge. They gather their views from other sources than the Scriptures; and, to use a common proverb, they strive to weave ropes of sand, while they endeavor to adapt with an air of probability to their own peculiar assertions the parables of the Lord, the sayings of the prophets, and the words of the

---

45   Irenaeus. Against Heresies. III. 3. 1-2.
46   Irenaeus. Against Heresies. III. 3. 2.
47   Irenaeus. Against Heresies. III. 3. 4.
48   Irenaeus. Against Heresies. III. 3. 4.
49   Irenaeus. Against Heresies. III. 12. 12.

apostles, in order that their scheme may not seem altogether without support. In doing so, however, they disregard the order and the connection of the Scriptures, and so far as in them lies, dismember and destroy the truth. By transferring passages, and dressing them up anew, and making one thing out of another, they succeed in deluding many through their wicked art in adapting the oracles of the Lord to their opinions.[50]

In other words, Irenaeus is saying that the heretics rip Scripture out of context and reinterpret them in ways the authors would never have approved, and then add material from other sources as well. This sounds amazingly like such ancient writings as the Gospel of Thomas! Sadly, this also sounds like the way some modern pastors treat Scripture!

In recent times many heretical writings, written around Irenaeus' time, have been discovered near a village in Egypt called Nag Hammadi. They prove that Irenaeus was absolutely right in his assessment above. People sometimes say or imply that the in the fourth century, church bishops "kicked out" these Nag Hammadi writings but this is simply ignorance or dishonesty. The church never "kicked them out," because the church never considered putting them in their New Testament in the first place!

The worldview of most Nag Hammadi writings is so nonsensical and diametrically opposed to that of the Old or New Testaments that discussing whether to include them in the New Testament would be like discussing whether the DaVinci Code or the Atheist Manifesto should be in the New Testament! If you doubt this, please purchase a copy of The Nag Hammadi Library and read them for yourself.

---

50   Irenaeus. Against Heresies. I. 8. 1.

One thing that is particularly interesting about Irenaeus is that he even writes of the "Old Testament" and "New Testament," and does so two hundred years before any church council met to discuss the issue. Irenaeus specifically includes Paul's letters in the New Testament. For example, Irenaeus writes,

"But why say I these things concerning the Old Testament? For in the New also are the apostles found doing this very thing, on the ground which has been mentioned, Paul plainly declaring..."

What follows are quotes from First Corinthians. Irenaeus continues, "If, therefore, even in the New Testament, the apostles are found granting certain precepts...."[51]

It is important to note that Irenaeus quotes extensively from Paul. In fact, so extensive are Irenaeus' quotes, it almost seems like the majority of the New Testament could be reconstructed from Irenaeus' quotes alone! He quotes from every one of Paul's letters except Philemon. This doesn't mean Irenaeus didn't think Philemon was Scripture, but probably just that Philemon was such a tiny letter that Irenaeus didn't have occasion to quote from it. And while many modern critics deny that Paul wrote such letters as First and Second Timothy, Titus, or Colossians, Irenaeus has no doubt that the author of all these letters was Paul.

Another striking thing about Irenaeus is that he doesn't write as if he's trying to convince people that the books of the New Testament are Scripture. He writes as if he just knows that the church everywhere will agree with him that these books are inspired, sacred Scripture.

The impression left by some modern writers that there was no New Testament before fourth century Christian bishops

---

met to discuss the issue is nonsense. While it is true that some of the smaller letters in the New Testament continued to be in dispute by a few churches into the fourth century (e.g. James, Jude, 2 Peter, 2 and 3 John) for the most part, the New Testament in general, and Paul's letters in particular, had been unanimously accepted by Christians as Scripture for over two hundred years before these councils met.

APPENDIX THREE

Jesus and Paul

Throughout history there have been those who thought that Paul was the corrupter of Jesus. In other words, they see Jesus as just a good Jewish teacher, or reformer, or revolutionary, or mystic (the critics can't seem to agree on which one) but they agree that he was not the Messiah, Savior or Son of God that Paul proclaimed him to be. Some deny that Jesus even *thought* of himself as Messiah, Savior or Son of God. The point of this chapter is to show that what the Gospels say Jesus taught about himself and his message, is the same thing that Paul taught about Jesus and Jesus' message.

The Christology[52] of Jesus

Christology is the theological study of Christ. There is no question that Paul claimed Jesus was the Son of God, Savior, and Israel's long awaited Christ (Messiah). Some of the more radical critics, however, like to deny that Jesus ever thought of himself in such lofty terms.[53] When it is pointed out that the

---

52   Christology is the study of the person and work of Jesus Christ from a theological perspective.

53   Marcus Borg writes, "But as the New Testament scholar John Knox argued a generation ago, thinking that Jesus thought of himself in such grand terms raises serious questions about the mental health of Jesus." And "Indeed, we have categories of psychological diagnosis for people who talk like this about themselves" (Borg, Marcus and N.T. Wright. *The Meaning of Jesus; Two Visions*. San Francisco : HarperSanFrancisco, 1998, 146, 149. Indeed, if Jesus was not who the Gospel writers say he claimed to be, it does raise questions about

gospels present Jesus as Messiah, for example, some critics will say that Jesus himself never claimed to be the Messiah or Son of God, but that this is just a claim the Gospel writers make *about* him.

But this is simply not true. In John 4:25, for example, Jesus was speaking to a Samaritan woman by a well when she told Jesus, "I know that the Messiah is coming (he who is called the Christ): When he comes, he will tell us all things." Jesus responded, "I who speak to you am he." Jesus was clearly claiming to be the Messiah.

The critics, however, will say that you can't really trust the Gospel of John because it was written so late (90's AD) and is so theological...as if being theological means it can't be historical! The same critics, however, will often rely heavily on the historian Josephus for historical background to the time in which Jesus lived, but Josephus wrote his book, *Antiquities of the Jews* about the same time John wrote his gospel!

Anyway, the Gospel of John is not the only gospel in which Jesus claims to be Messiah, Savior or Son of God. In Mark 14:61-62, when Jesus was on trial, the high priest asked him, "Are you the Christ, the Son of the Blessed?" (i.e. the Son of God. Pious Jews would often use another word like "blessed," "heaven" or "Power" to avoid saying the name God). Jesus responded very clearly saying, "I am." There is nothing ambiguous about that, and most scholars believe that the Gospel of Mark was the earliest of the four Gospels to be written.

Jesus continued, "And you will see the Son of Man seated at

---

his mental health. In fact, perhaps that is why his enemies charged him with being insane or demon possessed! This is why some Evangelicals have argued that Jesus was either a liar, lunatic or Lord. The idea that he was just a good Jewish teacher or mystic is not open to us.

the right hand of Power [God], and coming with the clouds of heaven."[54] This is a reference to a passage in Daniel 7 in which Daniel has a vision about "one like a son of man" who "came to the Ancient of Days" (God) "with the clouds of heaven." God gave to this son of man "dominion and glory and a kingdom, that all people, nations, and languages should serve him; his dominion is an everlasting dominion which shall not pass away and his kingdom shall not be destroyed."[55]

In the Gospel of Mark, Jesus claims to be this son of man, this king to whom an eternal kingdom is given. This is Messiah language, as Jesus' enemies understood quite well. In Mark, for example, Pilate asks Jesus, "Are you the king of the Jews?"[56] Pilate then asks the crowd, no doubt sarcastically, "Do you want me to release for you the King of the Jews?"[57] Pilate asks the chief priests what he wants them to do with "the King of the Jews."[58] The soldiers mocked him saying, "Hail King of the Jews."[59] Pilate ordered the inscription over Jesus' cross to read, "The King of the Jews."[60] This is Messiah language. Jesus' enemies clearly understood that Jesus was claiming to be the Messiah, the true King of the Jews.

Many critics will no doubt respond that all of this Messiah, Son of God talk did not really go back to Jesus but was just part of the "encrusted tradition" added by the later church. But among the critics' own criteria for determining what is historically reliable is a principle known as "multiple independent attestation." Multiple independent attestation simply means that we have more reason to trust events or sayings that are attested in more than one independent

54   Mark 14:62
55   Daniel 7:13-14
56   Mark 15:2
57   Mark 15:9
58   Mark 15:12
59   Mark 15:18
60   Mark 15:26

source. Even the critics view Mark and John as independent sources and both Mark and John unambiguously present Jesus as claiming to be Messiah. This is precisely how Paul viewed Jesus as well.

It should be noted, however, that there were numerous messiah wannabees in those days and Jewish leaders did not seek to execute people just because they claimed to be a messiah. It was Jesus' much more radical claims that led to his execution. For example, when Jesus rode into Jerusalem on a donkey (recorded in all four Gospels), Jesus was deliberately fulfilling a prophecy from the book of Zechariah which says, "Shout aloud, O daughter of Jerusalem! Behold, your king is coming to you; righteous and having salvation is he, humble and mounted on a donkey...."[61]

This is certainly a messianic passage but may be more than that. In the context of Zechariah, Israel's king is none other than God! In Zechariah, God promises, "I will dwell in your midst, declares the LORD"[62] [Yahweh, the name for God], and The LORD [Yahweh] will be king over all the earth.[63] Jesus was deliberately presenting himself as the fulfillment of prophecies about God, Israel's true King, coming to His people.

The idea that Jesus presented himself as the fulfillment of prophecies about God coming to His people is supported by Jesus' own words and actions in Mark 2:5 where Jesus heals a paralyzed man saying, "My son, your sins are forgiven." In a first century Jewish context (and context is everything), only God could forgive sins!

Some critics try to dance around this claiming that Jesus was not actually claiming to forgive sins directly, but only pronouncing forgiveness like a priest would pronounce God's

61   Zechariah 9:9
62   Zechariah 3:11
63   Zechariah 14:9

forgiveness. But according to Mark, Jesus' critics knew exactly what he was claiming. They said, "He is blaspheming! Who can forgive sins but God alone?"[64] The writer of the Gospel of Mark clearly wants us to understand that Jesus was putting himself in the place of God—and that Jesus did amazing miracles to back up his claim.

A little bit later, Jesus healed a man on the Sabbath Day when, according to God's law in the Old Testament, no one was supposed to work. When Jesus was challenged about this, he defended his actions from Old Testament Scripture, but then added, that "the Son of Man is lord even over the Sabbath."[65] In a Jewish context only God was over Sabbath! Jesus was claiming authority that properly only belonged to God. No wonder his enemies were furious and thought he was a blasphemer!

The point of all this is that the Synoptic Gospels (Matthew, Mark and Luke) all present Jesus as proclaiming himself to be the Messiah, Savior and Son of God. This is the same view of Jesus presented by the Gospel of John and it is the same view of Jesus presented by Paul. In other words, Paul was not making up some new doctrine or mythology about Jesus. Paul was simply teaching about Jesus what Jesus had already taught about himself.

The Soteriology[66] of Jesus

Soteriology is the study of salvation. Paul taught that Jesus' death on the cross provided the atoning sacrifice for our sins and that salvation was solely by God's grace, apart from any human works or merit, through repentance and faith in Jesus

---

64   Mark 2:7
65   Mark 2:23-28
66   Soteriology is the study of the doctrine of salvation

Christ. [67] As seen below, Jesus taught the same thing.[68] What Paul explained with logical arguments, however, Jesus often taught in stories.

Jesus told a story about a Pharisee and tax collector who went to the temple to pray. Pharisees were highly respected religious leaders while tax collectors were often viewed as despicable traitors who would pad their own pockets while collecting taxes for the occupying Roman enemies. Luke 18 records the Pharisee as praying:

"I thank you, God, that I am not a sinner like everyone else, especially like that tax collector over there! For I never cheat, I don't sin, I don't commit adultery, I fast twice a week, and I give you a tenth of my income"
.

The tax collector, on the other hand, "beat his chest in sorrow, saying, 'O God, be merciful to me, for I am a sinner.'"[69] Jesus said it was the tax collector, not the religious leader, who went away right with God. The point seems to be that God accepts those who come to him in humble repentance, acknowledging their sinfulness before God and seeking his mercy, rather than those who self-righteously think their goodness gains them merit before God. This was exactly the message that Paul taught. Paul insisted that if people are saved it is all because of the grace of God and has nothing to do with any human merit or works on our part.[70]

Jesus told another story about a landowner who went out to the marketplace early in the morning to hire workers for a day in his fields. He and the workers agreed on the normal daily wage. Later, at nine o'clock, the landowner went again to the marketplace to hire more workers, promising to pay them

67   Romans 3:21-25; 5:9
68   Matthew 19:28-29; John 6:51-53
69   Luke 18:11-13, NLT
70   Romans 3:27-4:4; Galatians 2:16; Ephesians 2:8-10.

the normal daily wage. He went out again at noon, and at three and at five, each time promising to pay the normal daily wage. At the end of the day, each worker received the normal daily wage as agreed, but the workers who were hired first complained. Those who had only worked an hour received the same pay as those who worked all day. That didn't seem fair. The owner replied that he paid everyone exactly what they had agreed and asked why they should be so angry just because he was kind to those who came later.[71]

Of course today the offended workers would probably file a lawsuit, but we have to remember that this was just a story to illustrate a point. The story is about God and the point seems to be that God rewards people not according to how long or hard they've worked, but according to his own grace. Those who turn to God shortly before death receive the same grace of salvation as those who labored for their whole lives. Is this unfair? Of course not since none of us deserved any of God's grace to begin with. This teaching is precisely in line with what Paul taught about being saved, not by works, but by God's grace through faith.

Another story of grace is the well known story of the prodigal son in Luke 15:11-32. A man's younger son asked his father for his inheritance even before his father was dead. The father agreed and the son left home and promptly squandered all the money on wild living and prostitutes. He ended up tending pigs for a living (a horrible fate in the opinion of most Jews of that day). He sank into such poverty that even the pigs' feed looked good to him.

He finally decided to return home and throw himself on his father's mercy, saying, "Father, I have sinned against both heaven and you, and I am no longer worthy of being called

---

71   Matthew 20:1-16

your son. Please take me on as a hired man."[72] Before he even got home his father saw him coming and, "filled with love and compassion," he ran out to greet his son, embracing him and kissing him while the son confessed his sin. The father then ordered preparations for a great feast saying that his son "was lost, but now he is found."

Meanwhile the man's oldest son was upset because he had been faithful to the father while the younger son was living in such decadence. The father assured the older son, "you and I are very close, and everything I have is yours. We had to celebrate this happy day. For your brother was dead and has come back to life! He was lost, but now he is found!"[73]

Regardless of whether this is a story of Israel returning from exile, as some modern scholars argue, or whether it is a story of individuals repenting of sin, in either case it is the story of God's gracious acceptance of unworthy sinners (whether individually or as a nation) who repent of their sins and return to their Father. Once again, this story illustrates perfectly one of the primary themes in Paul's letters, i.e. God's gracious acceptance of repentant sinners, not because the sinners deserve acceptance, but solely because of the Father's grace.

Jesus' message, however, is not just about people repenting and turning to the Father, it is about people turning to *Jesus* in faith. The Gospel of John, of course, makes this very clear. For example, Jesus says, "I assure you, anyone who believes in me already has eternal life."[74] Later Jesus speaks of "his sheep" saying, "I give them eternal life, and they will never perish...."[75]

---

72   Luke 15:18-19
73   Luke 15:11-32
74   John 6:47
75   John 10:28

The fact that Jesus believed that he was the way to eternal life, however, is not just taught in the Gospel of John. According to both Matthew (19:16-30) and Luke (10:25-37), a man came to Jesus asking what he had to do to earn eternal life. Testing him, Jesus recited the commandments for him and the man responded saying that he had kept them all. Jesus replied, "There is still one thing you lack...Sell all you have and give the money to the poor, and you will have treasure in heaven. Then come, follow me."

What an unusual demand. Jesus apparently didn't tell everyone to sell all they had. When Zacchaeus, for example, repented and offered to give half of his goods to the poor, rather than chastise Zacchaeus for not giving all he had, Jesus commended him. Numerous wealthy women, supported Jesus and he apparently hadn't told them to sell everything. There is no evidence that he ever told the wealthy Joseph of Arimathea to sell everything.

Nor did later Christians understand Jesus to have made this a command for everyone. For example, Ananias and Sapphira (in the Book of Acts) were not condemned because they held money back, but because they lied in an apparent attempt to make themselves look good. There is no reason to believe that Paul demanded that the wealthy business owner, Lydia, sell everything either.

We could go on, but the point is to ask why Jesus made such an unusual demand of this rich inquisitor? The man was seeking eternal life, thinking he had kept all the commandments. Jesus was apparently testing him on the very first commandment, "You shall have no other gods before me." When the rich man demonstrated that he valued his riches more than he valued Jesus, the gospel writers want us to understand that this rich man had not even kept the first commandment, much less all of them. Jesus was not teaching that you can be saved by keeping the Ten Commandments, but was demonstrating that this man had not done so. In any event, the man came to Jesus wanting to know how to have eternal life and Jesus answer was, "follow me." Jesus taught that he was the way to eternal life just as Paul taught that Jesus was the way to eternal life.

In yet another example of repentance, faith and grace,[76] a Pharisee invited Jesus to eat in his home. Jesus, the Pharisee and the other guests were reclining at dinner. For more formal meals people often laid on their sides on the floor in a circle with their heads propped up on their left hand while they ate with their right. Everyone's legs were extended outward in a "U" shape with the food in the center. A woman of the city "who was a sinner", probably a prostitute, came in with very expensive ointment. She knelt down and as she began anointing Jesus' feet she began weeping. She "began to wet his feet with her tears and wiped them with the hair of her head and kissed his feet and anointed them with the ointment."[77]

The village was probably one of those places where everyone knew everyone, and everyone knew who this woman was. Purity was a big deal in that culture and for a rabbi to be touched by a sinner, especially a woman, was scandalous and the guests started murmuring against Jesus for allowing this to go on. Jesus reminded the Pharisee that when he came into his house, the Pharisee did not even extend to Jesus the common cultural courtesies of their time, but this woman had kissed and anointed his feet!

What Jesus said next undoubtedly shocked the guests: "I tell you, her sins, which are many, are forgiven-for she loved much." Then, speaking directly to the woman he said, "your sins are forgiven." Stunned, the guests murmured, "Who is

---

76   Luke 7:36-50
77   Luke 7:38

this, who even forgives sins?" Then Jesus said to the woman, "Your faith has saved you; go in peace."[78]

Wait a minute! Back the train up! Who said anything about faith? There was not a single mention of faith in this entire story until the very last sentence. What faith? The story is about sin and repentance—the woman was a sinner who was weeping, apparently over her sin. The story is about devotion—the woman showed a remarkable devotion to Jesus. The story is certainly about love—Jesus says the woman loved much and her actions showed how much she loved Jesus. But who said anything about faith?

The woman's repentance, love and devotion toward Jesus is precisely what saving faith is all about! There is a cute little children's song that says, "faith is just believing what God says he will do." Nonsense! The book of James says "even the demons believe...and tremble." Of course faith involves believing certain facts about Jesus—after all, the woman did not come to Jesus because she thought he was just another Pharisee! But saving faith is more than just believing certain doctrines. It is about a radical change of heart about who we are (sinners worthy of death) and who Jesus is (our Savior and only hope). This is precisely what Paul taught about faith and salvation.

There are, however, a few sayings and stories in the gospels that have led some Bible teachers to think that Jesus actually taught a form of salvation by doing good works. For example, Jesus tells a story of the final Judgment when the "sheep" will be separated from the "goats." In this story, "sheep" are those who feed the poor, help the sick, visit those in prison, etc. The goats are those who don't do any of those things.[79] But a closer examination of the story reveals that those who

---

78   Luke 7:49-50
79   Matthew 25:31-46

fed the poor and did other good works in the story, *did not do so in order to be saved* (they said, Lord, when did we ever see you in need and help?).

Paul teaches that while works do not save us, genuine saving faith results in a change of behavior.[80] This is precisely what Jesus taught.

The Ethics of Jesus

So both Jesus and Paul taught that saving faith produces a change in behavior. Both also agreed on the kind of behavior that faith, or more accurately, the Spirit produces. Both Jesus and Paul taught that we should love our neighbors as ourselves.[81] Both taught that we should even bless those who curse us[82] and that we should forgive those who wrong us.[83] Both Jesus and Paul taught the importance of honesty[84] and making peace.[85] Both taught that we should be compassionate,[86] that we should honor father and mother,[87] and care for those in need.[88]

Jesus said that if anyone sues you for your tunic let him have your cloak also.[89] Paul taught the same basic principle to the Corinthians when he told them not to take a fellow Christian to court before non-Christians but rather suffer the loss.[90]

---

80   Romans 6:1-2; cf. 6:15-16; Ephesians 2:8-10.
81   Matthew 22:39-40; Mark 10:28-31;Galatians 5:14;
Romans 13:9.
82   Luke 6:27-29;Romans 12:14
83   Matthew 6:14-15; 18:21-22;Colossians 3:13; Ephesians 4:32
84   Matthew 5:33-37; Colossians 3:9
85   Matthew 5:9; Romans 14:19
86   Matthew 5:7; 15:32; Colossians 3:12
87   Matthew 15:4; Matthew 19:19; Ephesians 6:2
88   Matthew 25:31-46; Galatians 2:10; Romans 5:26;
1 Timothy 5:8
89   Matthew 5:40
90   First Corinthians 6:6-7

When questioned about paying taxes to Caesar, Jesus said to give to Caesar what belongs to Caesar.[91] Paul said to give to those that which belongs to them and specifically mentions taxes.[92]

Contrary to many who think it is judgmental to talk about sin, both Jesus and Paul had a lot to say about sin. Of course they both condemned what we might call the "big" sins outlined in the Ten Commandments' like murder,[93] adultery,[94] and theft.[95]

But for both Jesus and Paul, sin was more than what we might think of as big sins. For example, both Jesus and Paul warned not only against murder but against unrighteous anger.[96] Jesus taught that we should bless those who curse us[97] and Paul taught the same.[98] Both Jesus and Paul preached not only against adultery, but against all sexual immorality,[99] even sensuality[100] and lust.[101] They didn't just preach against theft, but against coveting[102] and greed.[103] In fact Jesus warned against focusing too much on earthly possessions at all[104] and Paul, similarly taught that the love of money was the

91   Luke 20:19-25
92   Romans 13:6-7
93   Mark 7:21; (Romans 1:29; 13:9
94   Matthew 5:27-30; Mark 7:21; First Thessalonians 4:5;
Romans 13:9
95   Mark 7:21; Ephesians 4:28
96   Matthew 5:21-26; Galatians 5:20; Ephesians 4:31
97   Luke 6:28
98   Romans 12:14
99   Mark 7:21; Romans 13:13
100   Mark 7:22; Romans 13:13; Galatians 5:19
101   Matthew 5:27-30; Mark 7:21; First Thessalonians 4:5;
Romans 13:9
102   Mark 7:22; Romans 1:29; Ephesians 5:3
103   Luke 11:39; First Corinthians 5:10-11
104   Matthew 6:19-21; Luke 12:16-21

root of evil.[105] Both Jesus and Paul taught against deceit,[106] slander[107] and divorce.[108] Both condemned arrogant pride and self-righteousness.[109]

Other Parallels

All of this, of course, does not exhaust the parallels between Jesus and Paul. For example, virtually all Jesus scholars acknowledge that a big part of Jesus' message was the kingdom of God.[110] Paul also taught about the kingdom of God.[111] Both Jesus and Paul called people to repentance,[112] both taught the importance of prayer,[113] and both warned against false prophets[114] or false teachers.[115]

Both Jesus[116] and Paul[117] called God "Abba," an affectionate term for one's Father. This wouldn't mean much if all Christians and Jews in the first century called God "Abba," but as far as we know it seems to have been very unusual to speak of God with such intimacy.

Jesus taught that we should love him more than even our

---

105   First Timothy 6:10
106   Mark 7:22; Romans 1:29
107   Mark 7:22; Ephesians 4:31; Colossians 3:8
108   Matthew 5:31; 19:8-9; First Corinthians 7:11-13
109   Mark 12:38-40; Matthew 23:25-33; First Corinthians 13:4; Second Timothy 3:2
110   For example, Matthew 4:17; Mark 1:15; Luke 9:60; John 3:3-5.
111   For example, Romans 14:17; 1 Corinthians 4:20; Galatians 5:21; Ephesians 5:5; Colossians 1:13; First Thessalonians 2:12; 2 Thessalonians 1:5; 2 Timothy 4:1.
112   Luke 13:1-5; 19:1-10; Romans 2:4; Second Corinthians 7:10
113   Luke 18:1ff.; Luke 6:12; Matthew 6:5-13; First Thessalonians 5:17; First Timothy 2:8
114   Matthew 7:15
115   Second Timothy 4:3
116   Mark 14:36
117   Galatians 4:6; Romans 8:15

father, mother, sister, brother, wife, children, etc.[118] Paul said that people are accursed if they don't love the Lord.[119] According to the Gospels, Jesus had a last supper with his disciples, that it was the New Covenant in his blood, and that his followers were to continue to practice it.[120] Paul referred to the same event in First Corinthians and tied it to the New Covenant.[121]

According Matthew 28:19 Jesus commanded his disciples to "Go therefore and make disciples of all nations...." Similarly Mark 16:15 records Jesus as saying, "Go into all the world and proclaim the Gospel to the whole creation."[122] Paul's entire ministry could be summed up as obedience to this command as he went into the world to preach the gospel to everyone, regardless of race, class, religion or national origin.

According to all four gospels Jesus taught that he would come back again.[123] Paul also taught that Jesus would come back again.[124] Jesus taught that there would be a day of judgment when people would have to give account to God for every careless word they speak.[125] Paul also taught that there would be a day of judgment when God would judge the secrets of people's hearts.[126]

---

118   Matthew 10:37; Luke 14:26
119   1 Corinthians 16:22
120   Matthew 26:26-29; Mark 14:22-24; Luke 22:19-20.
121   First Corinthians 11:23-27.
122   Although most critics deny that Mark 16:9-20 was part of the original Gospel of Mark since it is missing from some early manuscripts, the church leader, Irenaeus (Against Heresies, 3.10.5?), quoted from this passage long before the production of the manuscripts in which this passage was missing.
123   Mark 13:24-26, 14:62; Matthew 24:30, 36, 44; 25:31; Luke 21:27; John 14:1-4.
124   First Thessalonians 1:10, 4:13-17; First Corinthians 15:23
125   Matthew 12:36
126   Romans 2:16

Conclusion

The point of this discussion is that while many people like to imagine that Paul was the corrupter of Jesus, the evidence actually shows that Paul was a faithful preacher of both Jesus and Jesus' message. Of course many critics, in their endless cynicism, will just argue that many of the teachings of Jesus recorded in the Gospels come, not from Jesus, but from "creative communities," i.e. early churches as they made up sayings to address problems in their churches.

But Paul suffered intensely for tenaciously preaching his message about Jesus. It is understandable that he would willingly expose himself to such suffering if he genuinely believed his message to be true. It doesn't make much sense to think that he was suffering so much—and drawing other believers whom he cared about deeply into that suffering as well—if he was just making up new doctrines as we went along. It is beyond the scope of this essay to address this point in detail but the reader who would like to pursue it further is encouraged to begin by reading Paul Wenham's excellent book, *Paul, Follower of Jesus or Founder of Christianity*[127] by David Wenham and *The Jesus Legend* by Paul Eddy and Gregory Boyd.[128]

---

127   Wenham, David. Paul; Follower of Jesus or Founder of Christianity? Grand Rapids : Eerdmans, 1995.
128   See also, Eddy, Paul Rhodes and Gregory Boyd. *The Jesus Legend.* Grand Rapids : Baker, 2007, 201-233.

APPENDIX FOUR

Works Cited

Borg, Marcus and N.T. Wright. (1998). *The Meaning of Jesus; Two Visions*. San Francisco : HarperSanFrancisco.

Eddy, Paul Rhodes and Gregory Boyd. (2007). *The Jesus Legend*. Grand Rapids : Baker.

Hagner, Donald. (1973). *The Use of the Old and New Testaments in Clement of Rome*. Leiden : E.J. Brill.

Hemer, Colin. (1990). *The book of Acts in the setting of Hllenistic History*. Winona Llake, IN : Eisenbrauns.

Irenaeus, *Against Heresies*. Ante-Nicene Fathers, vol. 1. Peabody, MA : Hendrickson, 1885.

Klingaman, William K. (1991). *The First Century*. New York : HarperPerennial.

Stott, John.(1994) *The Message of Acts*. Downers Grove, IL : Intervarsity Press.

Wenham, David.(1995). *Paul; Follower of Jesus or Founder of Christianity?* Grand Rapids : Eerdmans.

ABOUT THE AUTHOR

Dr. Dennis E. Ingolfsland, MA, MALS, DPhil, has published over 50 book reviews and 30 articles in such journals as the Journal of the Evangelical Theological Society, Princeton Theological Review, Trinity Journal, Christian Research Journal, Bibliotheca Sacra, as well as in popular magazines including Alliance Life, Facts for Faith, Christian Librarian, et al.

Dr. Ingolfsland has a bachelor's degree from Calvary Bible College with a double major in Bible/Theology and in Biblical Languages; two master's, one in Library Science from the University of Missouri at Columbia and the second in Theological Studies from Fuller Theological Seminary, and a Doctor of Philosophy (D.Phil.) from Oxford Graduate School (TN).

Director of Library Services and a full, tenured, Professor of Bible at Crown College, Dr. Ingolfsland also serves as the pastor of ValleyView Baptist Church in Shakopee, MN.

THE LEAST OF
THE APOSTLES

ISBN 978-1-935434-22-1

AN IMPRINT OF
GLOBALEDADVANCEPRESS
WWW.GLOBALEDADVANCE.ORG

www.ingramcontent.com/pod-product-compliance
Lightning Source LLC
Chambersburg PA
CBHW070757100426
42742CB00012B/2174